HOW MONEY WORKS

Secrets from the Other Side!

W. Scott Blackmon, CPA

ISBN 978-1-64471-401-0 (Paperback)
ISBN 978-1-64471-402-7 (Digital)

Copyright © 2019 W. Scott Blackmon, CPA
All rights reserved
First Edition

All rights reserved. No part of this publication may be reproduced, distributed, or transmitted in any form or by any means, including photocopying, recording, or other electronic or mechanical methods without the prior written permission of the publisher. For permission requests, solicit the publisher via the address below.

Covenant Books, Inc.
11661 Hwy 707
Murrells Inlet, SC 29576
www.covenantbooks.com

Table of Contents

Introduction 5
1—What is ACH and how does it work? 7
2—Do I need a budget? 13
3—What do I need to know about buying a car? 20
4—Why are checks still around? 25
5—Is cosigning for a loan a good idea? 27
6—How do Credit Cards work? 29
7—What are credit reports and credit scores? 37
8—How do debit cards aka check cards work? 43
9—How do I manage my debt? 51
10—When should I buy a house? 61
11—Do I really need life insurance? 65
12—When should I start saving for retirement? 68
13—How do I save money? 71
14—What do I need to know about the employer side? 74
15—Are there different kinds of banks? 78

Introduction

A secret is something that is not known by someone. Usually a real secret contains information that can be useful to the one who does not know it. The purpose of this book is to inform the reader of many things about money that they may find useful. The best way to learn secrets or anything else is to ask questions. This is why the chapters of this book all use questions as their titles. There are many types of questions and many types of answers. Answers can normally come in the short form or long form. Sometimes all you want is the short answer and sometimes you need more detail that is contained in the long answer. For this reason, and so it can be used as an ongoing reference guide, both the short answer and the long answer have been included in each chapter. This book is meant to help anyone with questions about the day-to-day aspect of personal finances. I believe it can especially help teenagers and young adults learn more about making decisions in the world of personal finance. I hope you find this book useful in improving your knowledge of money and how it works.

What is ACH and how does it work?

| The short answer: |

ACH stands for automated clearinghouse or automated clearinghouse. It is a system or an electronic network used in the United States to deposit or withdraw funds directly from your checking or savings account at a financial institution (normally a credit union or bank). This can also work with loan payments.

| The long answer: |

There are two major types of ACH processors. They are ACH receivers and ACH originators. Almost all financial institutions are ACH receivers and will process an ACH file that they received by depositing funds or withdrawing funds from an account per the instructions of the ACH file. ACH originators are the financial institution or other financial processor that creates the ACH file.

Then there is the middleman. In most cases, the middleman is the Federal Reserve Bank. When an ACH is created by the ACH originator, they send the file, normally with many other files, in a batch to the Federal Reserve Bank. Each individual file has information and instructions on it. Along with the information about the file itself, such as when it was created, who the ACH originator is, and the batch identification, the information would include the bank or the credit union that should receive the ACH file and the account number that will be affected by the ACH file. The Federal Reserve Bank sorts all the batch information it receives and then, using the nine-digit routing number of the bank or the credit union that should receive the file, creates a batch for that financial institution and sends the ACH batch with the individual ACH files. For research purposes and using a very secured method, the Federal Reserve Bank will allow banks and credit unions access to file data that affect their financial institution and provide a summary page of all the information related to each ACH file. This summary page is called the ACH detail.

Many people have heard of direct deposit. This is where employees normally provide a voided check, or the information listed on the bottom of their check to their employer, so the employees' pay can be deposited directly to their checking accounts. This type of transaction is called an ACH credit because the funds are credited to the account. Many employers require direct deposit because it reduces the costs to the employer of running the payroll process. Another type of ACH credit would be your tax refund from the federal government or your state government. The routing number of your bank or credit union and the account number you would like the funds deposited into is required, normally as part of your tax return, for this to work. One major thing to know about ACH, especially with ACH credits, is that your financial institution is sent the information in the ACH file for the deposit prior to receiving the funds for the deposit. This is why you may be able to see online how much your payroll deposit is on Thursday when you don't get paid until Friday. The bank or credit union does not receive the funds earlier than you do even though it can appear that way.

One of the most common uses of ACH in everyday life is with online bill payment systems. These are the most common types of ACH debits. They are called this because the funds are debited or withdrawn from your account. This can be through the online banking system at your bank or credit union or directly with the company you are paying. When using the online bill payment system provided by your financial institution, they already have half the information they need. This is the half that includes your account information or where the money is coming from. You still need to provide them the second half or where is the money going. When paying a single bill directly through the company online system, the opposite is true. They know where the money is going and you need to provide the information of where it is coming from. In other words, you have to give them the routing number of the bank or credit union and your individual account number that the funds are coming from.

ACH debits are very popular among large retailers that take checks. For example, if you write a check at a large grocery store chain, they may give you the check back after processing it through a digital reader. This reader has collected the data on the check. This would include the routing number of the bank or credit union, your account number at that financial institution, and the check number. These items are preprinted on your checks with magnetic ink that make the information easier for the scanner to read. The amount most likely would be collected from the input from the cashier since the other information is not handwritten like the amount. This is why even with the ACH process, a check that has been converted to an ACH transaction can still clear for the incorrect amount. This information may be included on your receipt. It is a good idea to compare the receipt to the check that was given back to you. This process allows for the retailer to receive your payment into their account much faster than the check processing procedures allowed in the past.

The conversion of a personal check to an ACH debit by a retailer is one example of a one-time ACH debit. There are a couple of other reasons a one-time ACH debit may post to your account. One of these is a person-to-person or P2P transfer. This has become very popular to use when funds need to be transferred from one person to another due to less cash being used for regular transactions. For example, if me and a friend go to lunch and I forget my wallet, I can pay him back for my lunch by using my mobile banking bill pay system or an app on my phone to complete a transaction for these funds back to him before we are done with lunch. The confirmation of this transaction can be sent to both of us before the ACH item file is even created. An impressive thing about this kind of software it that the financial institutions use other information other than account information to determine where the funds should be deposited. Another reason for a one-time ACH debit is to make a purchase or a one-time bill payment online. Some online retailers will allow you to enter your personal checking account information instead of a credit card number to complete an online purchase. Some will even save this information like they save your credit card information for future purchases. They want to make buying from them as easy as possible, but prefer to debit your checking account with an ACH because the processing of your purchase is cheaper for them using ACH rather than a credit card.

Person-to-person or P2P transactions are one way that ACH items have started to become quicker. A normal ACH file can take about three days to complete. These types of files are sent through the entire system about four times a day. This is the file information and not the funds related to the transaction. The funds are transferred between the ACH originator, the Federal Reserve Bank, and the ACH receiver on the settlement date. The settlement date is the date that all the money evolved in a batch of ACH should post on both sides of the transaction, including the personal account of the account holder at a bank or credit union. Another way ACH transactions are becoming quicker is the introduction of same-day ACH. This allows an ACH originator to send and settle the transaction on the same business day. These transactions are a little more expensive to create and transmit than a regular ACH. This cost is normally passed on to the customer requesting the same-day transaction. In some cases, it may be worth the cost to the customer if it prevents a returned item on the other end that would cost much more.

Many businesses will pay each other or accept ACH deposits as a method of payment. This can be a little risky because your account number can end up all over the place. And by place, I mean the world. Banks and credit unions have come up with a way to avoid this risk and maintain the simplicity of an ACH transaction. They do this with dummy accounts that only accept ACH credits and not ACH debits. Using this method, the business seeking payment can give their customer or vendor the dummy routing number and account number, and when it is received at the bank, they will match the dummy account to the real account for deposit. Any ACH debits or withdraws sent to this dummy account will exception out and be returned. This is possible because many financial institutions can and do have more than one routing numbers. Routing number are also called ABA routing numbers. ABA stands for American Bankers Association. Routing numbers in the United States are nine digits long, while in Canada they are eight digits long. Any routing number can be searched on the internet, and you can find out who owns it. This is public information in the United States.

At this point, you may be thinking: Who pays for all of this? The key point to remember is that ACH pricing is based on transaction volume and not the dollar amount involved. The higher the volume of transaction, the lower the cost per transaction depending on the ACH contract agreements between the parties involved. The cost of sending a one cent ACH transaction and a million-dollar ACH transaction is basically the same. The start of an ACH request comes from the customer of the ACH originator. The ACH originator will charge their customer a rate per ACH file. This rate can change based on the volume. For example: the first 10,000 ACH files for a month may be at a rate of $0.01 per file, but any additional files could be at $0.005 per file. Depending on the contract agreement between the ACH originator and their customer, there can be many different rate tiers. Next comes the middleman's cut. The Federal Reserve Bank will charge the ACH originator for sending them the files and distributing the ACH file information to the appropriate ACH receiver. The Federal Reserve Bank will also charge their fees on a tier-based structure. Then comes the middleman's second cut. The Federal Reserve Bank also charges the ACH receiver for delivering the ACH files. The ACH receiver normally does not charge any fees for receiving and posting the transactions in the ACH files. The exception to this is if the ACH receiver is required to do research to find the correct account for posting of the ACH item, a charge could be applied. The item could also just be returned to the ACH originator with a code that tells the ACH originator that the account could not be found. Most fees to account holders are related to inefficient funds in the account for ACH debits. This is similar to a returned check fee for bouncing a check. One of these fees can cover the cost of processing a high number of ACH items.

There are three major points to remember about ACH transactions. They are the order of processing, returns and disputes, and your account information. The standard practice for most financial institutions (banks and credit unions) is to post the credit ACH transactions before the debit ACH transactions for any given settlement date. This is done to be friendly to the account holder and minimize return processing. It also results in fewer complaints about return fees from account holders. This practice may become more difficult as same-day ACH item processing becomes more popular and more cost effective for ACH originators. The main item to remember about the returns and disputes of ACH transactions is that they can be processed as easily, if not more so, than a disputed check that cleared for the wrong amount. Even though a check converted to an ACH transaction may not have the image of the check, it can still be returned if it clears for the incorrect amount. Please check your account holder agreement with your financial institution for limitations and time limits. These time limits may be based on the date of the transaction or on cutoff date of the last monthly statement. These types of errors are happening less and less frequently due to the increase of digital scanning, but many ACH originators still hand key items and this can lead to errors. The last and probably the most important thing to remember about ACH transactions is that from the beginning to the end of the transaction, and everywhere in between, everyone in the process has your account information. They have the routing number of the bank or credit union where your checking account is located and they have your account number itself. When you write a check to a big box store or pay your credit card bill by sending in a check, or even using online bill pay, depending on the format, your information goes through many computers that belong to many different financial institutions and the Federal Reserve Bank.

Do I need a budget?

The short answer:

This may be one of the easiest, if not the easiest, of all the short answers. The answer is *yes*. If money is tight, then you need a budget. If you don't want to waste money, then you need a budget. If you want your money to work the best way for you and as efficiently as possible, then you need a budget. It does not matter how much money you have; I can't think of many people who don't fit into one of these three categories, can you?

The long answer:

If you want to get control of your money, a budget is a very good place to begin. If you already use a budget, then you have already begun the process of assessing your financial situation. Tracking where your money is going and planning to spend a certain amount on certain things is most likely more than most people are doing. That will change as things get tighter and tighter financially. When things get more expensive across the board, people will be forced into watching their funds more and more closely.

The next step is categorizing or grouping your expenses by type. I would recommend two large types and then depending on your personal circumstances, breaking down those type into smaller subgroups. The two large types would be needs and wants. Wants could also be called luxury items. A few examples of needs would be things that you have to have such as food, medicine or medical expenses, clothes, rent or mortgage. A few examples of wants would be entertainment, such as cable or satellite TV, going out to eat, and grown-up toys such as the latest and greatest electronic devices and apps. Please notice that I did not place internet access into either of these groups. That is because the internet can be used for so many things it actually would fit into both categories. It is used for entertainment and therefore would fit into the wants type of expense. However, the internet can be used as a great tool for keeping track of your money and be a good tool for also saving money. This would make the internet very useful for supporting lowering the costs of items that would fit into the needs type of expenses. Depending on how you would choose to use internet access would determine which type of expense it would be on your budget.

If you are not currently using a budget, then now is a great time to start. Using the information provided in the previous two paragraphs, your monthly bills, and the following quick budget chart below, you can create your own budget and start using the information to help you assess your current financial situation. Don't be concerned if the chart does not match your monthly bills. Add and take away what you may need; everyone's household expenses are different and can fluctuate. The chart is a monthly budget based on two people each earning two biweekly paychecks per month. The items listed are generic in nature, but when making your budget, you may want to list each expense by the payee.

HOW MONEY WORKS

INCOME SECTION			
	Net Amount	Checks Per Month	Monthly Amount
Net Paycheck #1	$1,250.00	2	$2,500.00
Net Paycheck #2	$ 500.00	2	$1,000.00
Total Net Monthly Income			$3,500.00
EXPENSE SECTION			
Need Expenses			
Rent or Mortgage	$1,500.00		
Vehicles	$ 430.00		
Groceries	$ 400.00		
Utilities	$ 250.00		
Gas	$ 300.00		
Savings - periodic	$ 100.00		
Savings - long-term	$ 300.00		
Total Need Expenses	$3,280.00		
Want Expenses			
Movies	$ 40.00		
TV	$ 100.00		
Restaurants	$ 80.00		
Total Want Expenses	$ 220.00		
Total of All Expenses	$3,500.00		
Total Net Monthly Income		$ 3,500.00	
Total of All Expenses		$(3,500.00)	
		$0.00	

Above is what most people would call a balanced budget. This means the total income and the total expenses are equal. Another thing that you may have noticed about the above sample is that "savings-periodic" and "savings-long term" are both listed as a needed expense. The periodic savings line item is because people don't buy certain things they needed every month. Some of these things would include clothes and medicine. These kinds of things should be accounted for every month and money should be set aside for them. The long-term savings line item is there to stress the importance of the mind-set of savings for big-ticket items, emergency needs, and a good personal safety net. The example above also fits in an additional safety net. It is based on two biweekly payments per month for the entire year. Well, if you are paid biweekly, you are paid twenty-six times per year and not twenty-four. Looking at these two additional paychecks in a different way can help with budgeting shortfalls, unplanned expenses, or other options depending on your priorities.

Most people use a budget to track their spending and don't pay that much attention to the revenue or income side. This makes perfect sense because normally you have more control over your expenses than you do your income. For example: you can choose to not have TV programing packages that are high-priced and whether you want the extra movie channels, but most people don't get to choose when they get a raise or how much it will be. This is where looking at your cash flow comes in. You not only have to be mindful of the funds going out, but of the funds coming in as well. People who work on commission, work a changing number of hours over a pay period, or work overtime every now and then have a good understanding about watching the funds coming in. If you have a salary or are hourly with the same number of hours every week, you may not look at the income side of a budget as closely because your net pay does not change. Due to increases in health care insurance and employers paying less or none of these increases, I would recommend watching the income side just as closely as the expense side of your personal budget.

There are also other reasons you could have the same rate of pay and your net pay could go down besides health care costs. These would include voluntary and involuntary items. A good example of a voluntary reason, or one that you approved your employer to take from your net pay would be an increase in your 401k contribution. There are many more examples of an involuntary reduction in your net pay. Among these are higher withholding tax rates for income taxes, Social Security taxes, or Medicare taxes. There is also the human element. Payroll is still run by a person somewhere. Even if they are just pushing a button, people make mistakes. The main point is to verify your paycheck, aka direct deposit, is correct; and if it changes, make sure you know why and can account for the change.

After you have a budget, make sure you can make adjustments to it. This would include new large dollar purchases that would have monthly payments such as a car or house. You can use this method to know how much you can afford in a monthly payment for a new item even before you start shopping for it. This will make the overall purchasing process quicker and easier. You can also use this strategy to back into the amount you may need for a down payment. A good guideline for a down payment on a large purchase where you will need to borrow the rest and make monthly payments is 20 percent.

Truly detailed budgeting includes more than just planning for income and expenses. It also measures on an ongoing or at least a periodic basis your assets and your liabilities. Your assets are the things you own, such as your cash on deposit in your checking and savings accounts, your house, your car, and even your retirement accounts. Your liabilities are the things that you owe. This would include your mortgage, your balance on your car loan, credit card balances, and bills that you have received, but not yet paid.

Here is where you may need to think like an accountant for just a little while. Your total assets minus your total liabilities is your net worth. You may hear on the news the term *net worth* used when they are talking about a very wealthy individual. It sounds like a term reserved for the rich, but it is not. It is just easier to calculate for the rich that own a lot of stock or other items of public record because their total assets are the only number used. The news and others would just assume that because the individual is rich they don't have any debt. This is not always the truth, and this is why they will say "estimated net worth." The fact is everyone has a net worth. It just takes some math to figure out what it is.

The best way to calculate your net worth is to do it as of a certain date. I would recommend at the end of a month. Some research may be needed for accurate values of assets such as your house or car. Using your assessed values for items that are taxed is a conservative and reasonable approach. If you only calculate it once a year, then I would suggest doing it in early January as of December 31. You may need to wait on items such as bank statements, retirement statements, and bills with balances due. An example is provided on the following page.

Personal Net Worth Calculation
As of Dec. 31, 20XX

Assets:			
	Cash on Deposit	$	2,000
	House	$	200,000
	Car	$	10,000
	Retirement	$	20,000
	Total Assets:	$	232,000
Liabilities:			
	Mortgage Balance	$	150,000
	Car Loan	$	3,000
	Credit Card balances	$	5,000
	Other bills	$	1,500
	Total Liabilities:	$	159,500
Net Worth:		$	72,500

The main thing to remember about budgeting is that the whole purpose of doing it is to be able to manage your money. If you don't manage your money, it will manage you!

What do I need to know about buying a car?

| The short answer: |

The short answer is that buying a car is one of the largest purchases, besides a home or education, that most people make. It is not just a transaction between you and the car dealer or any other seller of a vehicle. This is usually a three-sided transaction. First there is you, the buyer of the vehicle, then there is the seller of the vehicle; and lastly, if you are getting a loan for the vehicle, like most people need to do when buying a car or truck, there is the lender of the funds for the vehicle. Also known as the lien holder.

| The long answer: |

Okay, now that you have the mind-set that there are three parties involved in this very important and expensive transaction, I would guess your first question would be: Where do I start? This is the logical question and the logical answer would be to start at the beginning. However, the beginning is not where you may think it is. If you need a car, you may think that you start where the cars are and go to a car dealer. This is correct and logical thinking for buying most items in your life, but for a car, most people will need to get a loan in order to buy a car. Because most people would need a loan to purchase a vehicle the beginning of the process of buying a car really should be at the lender and not the car dealership.

The first place to start, after deciding some personal preferences such as the kind of car you need and the make you may like best, is to find a good lender. This could be someone you know that works for a bank or credit union or just the lender that gives you the best interest rate on the loan. Remember that the interest rate is very important. You are not just paying for the car you're buying. You are also paying for the money you are borrowing to purchase the car. The price of the money you are borrowing is represented by the interest rate the lender will charge you for the borrowed funds. Shopping interest rates at potential lenders is as important as shopping dealerships for the best deal. Most lenders will provide two sets of interest rates for vehicles. One for new cars and one for used cars. New cars used to be cars that had not been titled to any one before the sale. Under this definition, nobody drives a new car except for the demo cars at a dealership. A more up-to-date definition of a new car is one that is three model years old or less. Every lender can define a new car differently, so be sure to ask when asking about rates, especially if you are looking for a "used" car that may not be very old.

Many lenders will have their interest rates posted online or if at a bank or credit union they will have them posted in the local branch. There is wording that normally comes with these posted rates. Some people may call it fine print. Look for the wording "as low as." This is a nice way of saying you can get this rate, but it comes with certain conditions. This sounds like it may be a bad thing, but it may not be a problem at all depending on the conditions and your personal preferences with dealing with finances. An example of one of these "as low as" conditions is you may be able to get a quarter of a percent (0.25%) reduction from the normal rate if you have your payment automatically deducted from your account each month. This is a very common condition because it increases the likelihood that payments will be made timely and therefore reduces the risk to the lender of the loan becoming delinquent or completely uncollectible. This deduction is normally done by an ACH transaction, if your account is at another financial institution. If you have your account and loan at the same bank or credit union as your primary checking account, they will most likely do an internal transfer of the loan payment. Either way the lender has access to your account information.

Some people may not like that, while other may see it just as the way a loan payment is done.

Another way of saying "as low as" is that the interest rate has a floor. In other words, no matter any other circumstances the rate will not be lower than this rate. For example: the normal rate may be 3.00% on the loan that you need, but the "as low as" rate, or the floor, may be 2.00% and lender has six conditions that will lower your rate by 0.25% each. You can only get the benefit of four of these six conditions, even if you achieve or agree to five or six of them. Some lenders may have conditions that will lower your rate by 0.50%, but there are not many of these and usually have to do with a down payment on the vehicle of at least 20% of the value of the car. This condition is not normally met by the borrower and even if it is some lenders will still only reduce the interest rate by 0.25%. Saving up for a 20% down payment is a good idea, if possible, because it means you will be borrowing less money and you will be more likely to get the loan you need for the vehicle you need.

When speaking with the lender, the bank, or credit union in most cases, your goal is to get "preapproved" for the loan related to the vehicle you would like to purchase. A number of topics will come up in the discussion. A few of these topics will most likely include the type of vehicle you want to purchase, the length or term of the loan in months, and the monthly payment amount you would like to pay. Notice I said: the payment amount you would like to pay and not the payment amount that you can afford. The lender will do calculations to figure how much they think you can afford when they gather other information. This information would include your total monthly income, your disposable income, and other debt and related payments that you have on your credit report. The more of this information you have before you start speaking with a customer service representative or loan officer the faster the process will go for you. Other information that could help you can be obtained by doing a little shopping for a lender. Check out their websites, most have lots of information about their different car loans and even calculators that will help you find out how much of a monthly payment that would fit into your budget. When using these calculators and running numbers for your budget remember to factor in other things that will not be included in them. Examples of these would be changes in your car insurance premiums, property taxes if your state has those for vehicles and changes in fuel costs.

    The lender is looking for many things to determine if they can approve you for the car loan or not. Keep in mind that they want to approve you and not decline you because they don't make any income from declining people. The first thing that comes to mind may be your credit score and that would be smart, but the credit score normally has more to do with the interest rate you are charged for the loan more than whether you get the loan or not. A second item the lender will be looking for is your disposable income. This is the income that you have not committed to other debt. For example, if you make $2,500 per month in salary or wages and you have a $1,500 mortgage and a $400 payment on another car that you are keeping after this new loan you would only have disposable income of $600 per month. Under these circumstances, the lender would not give you a loan that would require you to make a $700 loan payment each month, no matter how good your credit may be. The math does not work in this scenario because there would not be enough income to pay all of the commitments and the loan would be too risky to make. The lender gathers this information from you and your credit report. Many of them will ask you before pulling your credit report for two reasons. The first is to run the calculation before pulling your credit report because each time your credit report is pulled it can lower your credit score if it is a hard pull. Please see the section on credit scores and credit reports about soft and hard pulls. The next thing the lender will look for is the amount of the loan compared to the value of the vehicle. Some lenders will give you a loan for more than a vehicle is worth up to a certain percentage of the value. You may wonder why would they do that. The main reason is to make it more likely to get your business. A secondary reason would be so additional items can be financed with the vehicle, such as nonfactory improvements. Some of these may include adding a sunroof or getting it painting differently before purchase. Even if a lender will give you a loan for more that the vehicle is worth, it is usually not a good idea. It will take you longer to pay off the loan and in the end cost you more to borrow the funds for the loan because you are financing a greater amount. A good idea is to put down 10% to 20% if at all possible. This will lower the loan to value ratio and make it more likely that you will be approved for the loan. It will also contribute to a lower monthly payment amount and lower finance charges (interest) over the life of the loan.

After the "preapproval" process with the lender, you will then be ready to start shopping for a vehicle. When doing this, you can use your "preapproval" status with the lender in a number of different ways. You can disclose this upfront when payment first comes up or you can wait until you start speaking about payment and options with the finance manager or not mention it at all. Your approach will be determined by your personal negotiation style and the salesperson you are dealing with. No matter how you decide to go with this, there are two things to remember. The first is the salesperson needs you more than you need them. You can always go somewhere else. The second and very important thing to remember is not to disclose how much you have been preapproved for. The finance manager is a salesperson as well and will try to get you to add on things you may not want or need. A couple of the items that the finance manager may try to sell you are MRC and GAP. The first one, MRC, stands for mechanical repair coverage and is an additional warranty on certain parts of the vehicle. The second item, GAP, is an insurance product that can cover the gap in normal insurance. For example, if your car is totaled and cannot be driven again and your normal automobile insurance company pays you (normally paid to you and your lender) $2,000 for the car, but your loan balance has $3,000 left on it, the GAP insurance will contribute to the remaining $1,000. Lenders love this insurance product because it helps reduce their risk on loans. Because of this, they will normally offer this product at a lower price than a car dealer. Both MRC and GAP have markups, but the markups are normally lower at a lending bank or credit union than at the dealer. For used cars, an MRC warranty should be considered, but remember, you do not have to buy it or the GAP insurance product from the dealer.

Why are checks still around?

| The short answer: |

Check are still around because of how they work. They are also still around because of the information they contain. They work with not only the amount they are written for but also with the ABA routing number and account number on the bottom of the check. This information tells the Federal Reserve Bank and other financial institutions how the transaction should be routed. This is the same information used for ACH (automated clearinghouse) transactions. The overall cost of processing a check transaction is still the cheapest way to move money from one account to another.

| The long answer: |

When I say the cheapest way to move money from one account to another, who do you think I mean it is cheapest for? It is not the banks, or the retailers, but for the consumer and the small business owner. There are many different ways to complete transactions, but unless your financial institution provides free online bill pay with your account, then it still, in general, will cost you more for the convenience of paying your bills electronically. For the small business owner, it means they do not have to pay interchange fees, the fees associated with debit card and credit card purchases. This can save the small business owner an estimated 3% or more per transaction, depending on the type of card being used for the transaction.

There are also personal reasons that checks are still around. For example: If you want to send some money to someone that is far way, it is a lot easier to mail a check. This is especially true if it is a one-time thing. You don't have to get account information and set them up in an electronic system when you will not be sending them money again.

Another reason you may want to use a check is that even though you may find it old-fashioned, checks still create a very good paper trail of a transaction. This mean there are multiple layers of proof that you actually did pay something. This is good for paying taxes or fees to the government. It can also be good for down payments on large purchases. The paper trail creates proof and supporting documentation with your records, the payee's records, and of course, the financial institution that pays and clears the check. You may even be able to look at a picture, front and back, of your check with your online banking after it has cleared. This would be great if you paid something and the payee says you didn't pay their bill. You can provide them the copy of the cleared check. The back of the check should have the deposit information on it. If you do find yourself in this situation, please do not e-mail the image of the check, unless it is a secure email system. It will still have the bank or credit union ABA routing number on it and your account number. I would consider this type of information the type you would not want to send over an unsecured method.

The last and the main reason I think checks are still around, and will be for some time, is that it helps the account holder maintain a certain level of control. It doesn't matter if you're old, young, or somewhere in between. Most people like to have as much control over their money as they can. With checks, you have control of the amount it is written for, the date it is written on, and with the signature, you have the control of it not really being a check until you sign it. If these are not enough, you can even stop it from being a check, by voiding it. You can even place a stop payment on it, and if it has not already cleared, the bank or credit union will return it, if and when, it is presented. Some financial institutions may let you place a stop payment on a check with their online banking for a much lower fee than in a branch. Be careful if you ever have to place a stop payment as they are not normally permanent. There may even be a set time for the stop to expire, but it should be able to be renewed. In my opinion, the human nature of control will keep checks around for a long time.

Is cosigning for a loan a good idea?

| The short answer: |

Cosigning for a loan can be a good idea or a bad idea. It depends on many factors. It would depend the type of loan, the amount of the loan, and who you are cosigning for. This is as serious as getting your own loan because you are equally as responsible for the loan payment as the person you are cosigning for. One definition of a cosigner is: a joint signer of a promissory note.

| The long answer: |

When talking about cosigning for another person, most people may think of car loans, but cosigning is not limited to only automobile loans. To fully understand what the act of cosigning involves I have included a more detailed definition of the act of cosigning. To cosign: the act of signing for another individual's debt obligation, which involves taking on a legal responsibility to make payment on the other person's debt should that individual default on any of the payments.

Having a cosigner is one way for individuals with income too low or credit history that is not very good to obtain a loan that they normally would not qualify for otherwise. When the loan is paid as agreed, the individual will then have a better credit history and may no longer need a cosigner for future loans or credit. The cosigner takes the risk and the responsibility of payments for the loan. They will also have the loan payment history appear on their credit report. This is where the big risk with cosigning becomes part of the equation. If you cosign for someone, say for a car loan, and they start missing payments, the first time you may hear about this is when the collection department gives you a call. At this point, your credit has already been damaged. If the primary loan holder is behind on the loan, so are you!

Another thing to consider when thinking about cosigning is your own debt. Everyone has a limited amount of debt they can mathematically carry. In other words, if you cosign for someone's loan, it may prevent you from getting your own in the future, just because that loan is counting toward your debt-to-income ratio. Different banks, credit unions, and other lenders have different internal policies, but if the cosigned loan increases your debt-to-income ratio too much, you may have to do more shopping for your loan than you wanted. When doing this, each lender will have to pull your credit report and this can affect your overall credit score depending on how it is done. If your credit score drops too much, you may still get the loan, but will most likely have to pay a higher interest rate than you would have if you did not cosign for the other loan.

So, the bottom line when it comes to cosigning for someone is *trust*. How much do you trust that the primary loan holder will be able to, and willing to, make the loan payments? One way of looking at this is to ask yourself if you had the funds, would you lend them the money they needed?

How do Credit Cards work?

| The short answer: |

Credit cards are one of the most powerful financial tools for consumers, merchants, and lenders. Most people understand the basics of how a credit card works. The consumer uses the credit card to make purchases and within a month or so they get a bill to pay for those purchases. This is only the part that most consumers see. There is much more to how credit cards work.

| The long answer: |

In this section, we will explain what credit cards can do for consumers, merchants, and lenders. Knowing more about how credit cards work and how to apply that knowledge can not only save you money, but can also help you make better decisions on how to spend your money.

| *Consumers* |

There are many different types of credit cards that have many types of tools for consumers. The main tool that almost all credit cards have is, if the bill is paid in full by the due date, no finance charges are applied to purchases within the current billing period. If the bill is paid in full and you do not have any finance charges or fees, this means you have used the credit card issuer's (the lender) money for free from the time you made the purchase to the time you pay the bill. This means during this time the money you used to pay the bill is still in your account working for you. Unfortunately, most people do not use a credit card like this and use it as a line of credit in which they carry a balance from month to month and pay interest on the balance that is carried forward to the next month.

Other tools that credit cards have that can benefit the consumer come in the form of rewards programs. These are normally accounted for and show up on the monthly credit card statement in the form of reward points. Some credit cards issuers (lenders) that have agreements with airline companies may issue and show their rewards in the forms of miles. The good news for consumers is that these rewards are based on the usage of the card in the terms of dollars and not the amount of interest, fees, or charges paid for using the card. The bad news will be explained in detail in the section on lender tools.

Points and/or miles cards can be used in a variate of ways depending on the card. Let's take the miles cards first. These cards normally give you miles for purchases you make with an airline. Some of these cards are now starting to give you miles for other purchases as well. This is because the airline and the card issuer both want you to use the card more often. These cards are good for individual consumers that fly on a regular basis, but the main target for these types of cards are businesses. Many businesses have salespeople that make many business trips a year. These businesses are the consumer in this case and see the miles card as a way of reducing travel expenses.

Next are the points cards. These cards can be very simple or very complicated. The basic idea of these cards is that the more you spend using a points card, the more points you receive. These points can be higher based on the type or merchant. For example, you may get double points if you use your card to make a purchase at a grocery store or maybe even triple points if you use your card to purchase gas for your vehicle. Where these types of cards can get complicated is some of them will change the type of merchants that get you extra points for time to time. This information may be found on your monthly credit card statement as well as your points earned information.

The term *points* may seem very generic, but there is a good reason for that. They can be used in many different ways. Many points cards have a website you can access to redeem your points. When redeeming these points, you can normally do so in many different ways. A few examples you may be able to do are the following:

1. "Buy" an item on the site with your points and have it shipped to you.
2. Redeem your points for a gift card.
3. Make a donation to charity.
4. Have a credit amount applied to your card balance.

It is a good idea, if you have one of these cards, to redeem your points every now and then because most do expire. Even if you are lucky enough to fine a card that does not have points, miles, or rewards that expire, please remember that the terms of the credit card agreement that you sign when you apply for the credit card can normally be changed at any time. The notification of the changes would normally come with your monthly billing statement and be in very small print. Most people beside those who work in the lending industry are not likely to read these notifications.

One of the most popular credit card tools for consumers are the cards that offer "cash back" rewards. This is also popular for the card issuers because it is popular among the consumers. When these types of programs started, they got a lot of attention because checks were set to the cardholder. Now they are still popular because they are very simple. The cardholder normally does not need to redeem anything. The cash back amount is normally automated and will show as a credit on the cardholder's statement.

There are many types of cards that have special rewards or benefits to them as well. For example, if you want to make a large purchase, some cards may give extra time to make payments before charging interest on that specific purchase. These types of purchases may include home furniture, appliances, or a vacation. Other cards may have higher cash back percentage rates for your favorite place to shop online. Some cards may even have special bonus points if you transfer a balance from another card to their card. An important item to note on balance transfers is that they work like a cash advance on your card, and there is no delay in the charging of interest.

Merchants

To help understand how credit cards are useful tools to merchants, we will give you a brief history lesson. Before credit cards, if someone needed to buy something on credit, they needed an account at each merchant, and it was the responsibility of the merchant to keep track of how much was owned to them by that individual. Some types of merchants will still do this. It is referred to as running a tab.

When credit cards started, the card issuers (the lenders) took on the responsibility of paying the merchant and keeping track of what was owed to them. This took away the concern of who the merchant could trust for future payments and made credit transactions much easier because they were not the ones granting the credit to the consumer. It also eliminated the keeping of credit transaction records. This was also a benefit to the average consumer because they did not have to convince every merchant they made purchases from to give them credit.

As technology advanced, credit card transactions also became easier and faster than cash or check transactions. This made things a lot more efficient and convenient for the merchant, but the increase in efficiency and convenience came at a price. This price came in the form of interchange fees. A merchant will pay a fee to the card processor that is equal to a percentage of the transaction. This fee is normally a very small percentage of the transaction. Different types of credit cards have different rates of interchange fees. Some cards have an interchange fee that is so high some merchants will not accept that card. Higher interchange fees can cut into a retailer's profit margin. Some merchants, especially government entities, will charge a processing fee for paying with a debit card or credit card. The reason is to cover the costs they pay for the processing of the transaction through the credit card network. These processing fees are part of an agreement they sign in order to be allowed to take the cards for payment. They may have a separate agreement for each type of card or go through a third-party processor, normally a bank, that can help them process more than one type of card. Another part of these type of agreements other than the interchange rate is they will not require a minimum transaction amount. So, if you see a sign by a register when you are making a small purchase that says you have to use cash for transaction under a certain dollar amount, that merchant is violating that agreement with the card processor.

To put interchange fees into prospective I will provide a historical point of view. In the 1970s, gas prices were very high due to international supply issues and credit cards had still not been used by the majority of the public for very long, so gas stations would have different prices for a gallon of gas depending on if you paid cash or if you paid with credit. This was in an effort for gas stations to avoid paying the interchange fees and to stay as competitive on their prices as possible. During the "great recession" that started in late 2008, this happened again but was presented or marketed differently. It was advertised as a cash discount. I believe it was presented to the consumer in this manner in an effort to not violate the credit card processing agreements, but the main goal was the same as before, avoid the interchange fees and keep the prices as low as possible in order to stay competitive.

The other benefit for retailers that take credit cards instead of running their own credit program with trusted customers is the quick receipt of funds. Merchants normally have the funds in their account the next business day for transactions done by credit card. This allows merchants a quicker incoming cash flow. Merchants then use this cash to resupply inventory that they are selling faster than they otherwise would.

Many merchants find credit cards very useful for completing sales transactions, but don't like paying the interchanges fees to the credit card processors and the banks that issues the credit cards. Because of this, many merchants have their own cards. When applying for one of these cards, the merchant will usually give you deal of some kind. For example, zero percent interest for six months or 10% off all of your purchases today. These cards not only cut out the middleman by making the merchant the issuer, they also give the merchant the control of the interest rate that is charged to the consumer using that card. These cards normally have some of the highest interest rates off all credit cards. If you must carry a balance on a credit card, always compare rates, but it would normally be a good idea to carry that balance on a card that is not a credit card issued by a retail merchant.

Another tool merchants will use with credit cards is the authorization codes. Have you ever wondered when you pay for gasoline at the pump, you have to get authorization before the total amount of your purchase is known or completed? This is because when you swipe the card at the pump an authorization code is requested and received from the credit card processor. This has to be done before you are allowed to start pumping your gas. When this request is made, an amount is also requested to verify there is available credit for the transaction. The amount normally authorized at a gas pump is only $1.00. When gas prices were really high, approaching $4.00 a gallon, this was changed to higher amounts. This caused many problems with debit cards, which will be discussed in the chapter on how debit cards work. After the transaction is completed, a request for payment is then made using the same authorization code, but with the final posting amount of the transaction. The amount does not have to be the same. This is a method also used by hotels. This is why when you check in to a hotel, the front desk clerk will ask for a card in case you have any additional charges or amenities during your stay. A couple of examples would be renting a movie in your room or a minibar and snacks in the room. A salon and spa facility or restaurant at the hotel may also be able to add your charges to your room. With the authorization code they obtained when you check in, the hotel does not have to ask for your credit card again. They just update the amount and use the same authorization code. Because amenities and other items you may purchase while staying at hotel can add up, the hotel may use the authorization code differently than a gas station. They may get a higher authorization amount than the total of the room charges. For some hotels, not all may get an authorization for the amount of four nights when you are only staying three nights. Another way would be to increase the authorization amount by a certain percentage of the expected charges. Because of this, it is almost always better to use a credit card at a hotel instead of a debit card. This will be explained further in the debit card chapter, but if you really want to see how this works, log on to your credit card's website between the time you check in and the time you check out of the hotel the next time you stay at one.

Lenders (Credit Card issuers)

Credit cards are very powerful tools for lenders. Most people may think that the only purpose of the credit card tool for lenders is to increase interest income on the unsecured loan balance on the card. While the interest income that lenders can earn is substantial, this is not the entire purpose of issuing credit cards. There is another source of income for the card issuers called interchange income.

Interchange income are the fees a merchant pays for the ability to take the credit card as a method of payment. These fees are paid as a percentage of each transaction and that percentage depends on the type of credit card. The fees are then split between the major credit card company, such as VISA and Mastercard, and the issuing bank or credit union.

Different types of cards have different interchange rates. This is why some merchants will not take certain types of cards because if the percentage is too high, it could be greater than the profit margin on any given product or service. For example, if you are selling an item for $100 and you only make $3 on a cash transaction, you would not want to take a credit card that has an interchange rate of 3% because at best you would only break even. Some merchants have a business model where they make very little on each transaction but have thousands and thousands of transactions. These types of merchants cannot afford to take credit cards with high interchange rates. They would not stay in business.

Interchange income is very important to credit card issuers. They know you will most likely be using some type of card to make purchases, and they want you to use their card. This is why they are willing to pay you in the reward points or cash back for using their card. Now, comes the bad news that was mentioned in the section on consumer tools. Nothing is free and the credit card issuers are not paying for these rewards, the merchants are not paying for these rewards, and after all the hoops are jumped through you, the consumer, are paying for the rewards. The merchants add the interchange fees into the cost of doing business prior to pricing their products. This is why the rewards from the card issuers are paid to the consumer as a percentage of the card usage because that is how the interchange fees are paid to them by the merchant. This also means that if you pay cash for an item, the merchant actually makes more income on that single transaction.

Examples:

1. A merchant buys an item for $90 and sells it at a retail price of $100. The customer pays the $100 in cash. This means the merchant has gross revenue of $10 on this one transaction.
2. A merchant buys an item for $90 and sells it for $100. The customer uses their credit card and pays the $100 retail price. The merchant pays a 2% interchange rate for the type of credit card the customer uses. This means the merchant will pay the credit card company $2 in interchange fees. Their gross revenue on this one transaction would then only be $8 instead of $10.

A few things to remember about credit cards: First, they are an agreement between you and the issuing financial institution, normally a bank or credit union. The credit card is a line of credit with them. Next, remember that if you use a credit card to get cash in any form, there is no delay of the charging of interest. Finance charges start on the day of the cash advance. This includes using a credit card at an ATM. Some issuers give you a PIN so you can do this. Interest rates on credit cards are higher than most other types of loans, and it is a good idea to try to use the card in a way that you can pay it off every month you receive a statement. Finally, when looking for what kind of credit card to apply for, shop around. Find a card that will match the way you want to use it. This may mean at least two or three different cards because not one card can do everything you may want or need your credit card to do. The chapter on managing your debit will have more useful information on credit cards.

What are credit reports and credit scores?

| The short answer: |

Credit reports are the credit history reports of your borrowing and repayment behavior. Credit scores are a rating given to measure the quality of your credit history as a whole and are mostly used to determine the interest rate charged for your loan by a lender, depending on the type of loan.

| The long answer: |

Credit reports have many types of information related to your credit history. Here is a list of some of them:

- What lenders you have applied for loans with.
- How much money you applied for.
- How much money the lender lent to you. This is not always the same as what you first asked for.
- The minimum payment you are required to make for each loan you currently have.
- The amount of the minimum payment.
- Your next payment due date.
- The loans that have been paid as agreed.
- Credit cards that have been closed and why they were closed.
- The number of times a loan has been delinquent 30 days.
- The number of times a loan has been delinquent 60 days.

- The number of times a loan has been delinquent 90 days.
- The number of times a loan has been delinquent 180 days or more.

The delinquent days are very important. Just because you had a loan that is no longer delinquent, this does not completely fix your credit history. Some people think that just because they consolidate all their delinquent loans into one new loan and pay off the old loans that their poor credit history goes away. This may help with improving someone's credit history, but it would just be the beginning. It will still take time and discipline. The delinquency history stays on the credit report for some time. Lenders use this to help assess the risk of giving you a loan. Your income and the possible fact that you have very little debt before the loan you are applying for does not really matter if you have a history of not making your loan payments in a timely manner. Remember, another name for a loan is also a "promissory note." When you sign this document, you are making a legal promise to make the loan payments as agreed. This is the main reason credit reports exist. The lender doesn't not really know you or if they can trust you with thousands of dollars. A person's credit report is the "verify" part in the old saying: "Trust but verify."

Credit reports normally come from one of three credit bureau companies that collect credit history data. These three companies are Equifax, Experian, and TransUnion. Here is where things get a little messy. Lenders do not always get information from all three credit bureaus. Lenders have to pay the credit bureau to get your data. Because of this, a lender may just use one credit bureau thinking that they don't want to pay three times for the same information. Here is where the other side comes in. The credit bureaus can also charge lenders for reporting to them. Because of this, smaller banks or credit unions may not report to all three of the credit bureaus. The big banks and other large lenders will normally report to all three credit bureaus and pull data from all three credit bureaus as well.

After a lender gets your data, they have many choices on how they use it. They can compare the data from each of the credit bureaus and use the ones that agree will each other and ignore the other. The lender can average the two or three if they use more than one. They can choose to use only the one they think gives them the best or most complete information. Remember, most lenders want to give you a loan, but also want to minimize the risk of default.

When it comes to credit scores, the lender has all the above options and more. The main point of the credit score is to determine the interest rate to charge you for the funds you are borrowing from the lenders. Most lenders give letter grades, A through E, to a range of credit scores, sometimes even an A+. The below charts are a couple of examples.

Credit Score Range	Paper Grade
700 and above	A
620 to 699	B
560 to 619	C
500 to 559	D
499 and below	E

Credit Score Range	Paper Grade
720 and above	A+
680 to 719	A
620 to 679	B
580 to 619	C
520 to 579	D
519 and below	E

A loan with an A grade would be referred to a A- paper. The other grades would be referred to in the same manner. This is important if the lender wants to sell the loan in the future. Although the paper grade is the main point for determining the interest rate of the loan, it is only the starting point most of the time. Internal policies regarding terms and discounts can change the overall rate of a regular loan, such as car loans. Normally longer-term loans could increase the loan rate while rates could be lowered by a small percentage for an automatic payment.

Remember your credit score is important to your overall "good credit," but it is not the whole story when it comes to applying for a loan. The behavior, good and bad, in your credit report directly affects your credit score and therefore it affects the interest rate you pay on your loans. Here are a few things that can hurt and help your credit report and your credit score. Some may be obvious.

Behavior that hurts your credit are the following:

- Not making your loan payment.
- Making your loan payment late.
- Having your loan sent to the collection department or a collection agency.
- Getting a court judgment against you. This is where the lender or their attorney takes you to court in order to get you to pay your loan.
- Maxed out credit cards or credit cards over the limit.
- Closing credit card accounts that you have had for a long time.
- Applying for multiple loans at the same time or in a short period of time. Each time is a "hard pull" of your credit information and can lower your score. This is also true when adding utilities to your home.
- Not having at least one credit card.
- Filing for bankruptcy. This can take seven years to come off your credit report.
- Paying utility, phone, or other household bills late.
- A bounced check that goes to collections for the check amount or the related fees.
- Not paying a parking ticket. If it is your car, then it will hurt your credit, even if you were not the one driving the car at the time.

Behavior that helps your credit:

- Make sure the data in your credit report is correct. If incorrect, contact the lender and the credit bureau with the incorrect information. Don't let up until it is corrected.
- Pay off your credit card balance each month.
- If you carry a balance on your credit card, make sure it is less than 20% of the credit limit.
- If you have poor credit and cannot be approved for a regular credit card, get a secured credit card. The bank or credit union will put a hold on the funds that equal the credit card limit.

| Tip and Tricks: |

I would also like to include some methods my wife and I have used in our personal finances. These ideas may not be something you think of at the time, but I hope by reading these it will help you think about them before you need them. Some of these methods of cash and debt management have helped us both have credit scores over 800.

The first and main thing we have done is limit the number of items we pay interest on. We have only paid interest on our house, our cars, and our student loans. This does not mean we do not borrow funds in other ways. The main example is not paying interest or finance charges on credit cards. We avoid these expenses by paying of credit cards monthly or taking advantage of zero percent finance charge offers. The card balance is paid off before interest begins. We also do not have any credit cards with an annual fee or get cash advances on a credit cards. Credit cards give you time to pay with no interest on regular purchases before finance charges are applied, but this is not this case with cash advances. Interest charges start immediately when you get a cash advance. This is why some credit card issuers will send you a PIN with your card. Getting cash from an ATM, using your PIN, with a credit card is a cash advance.

Another way to take advantage of zero percent finance deals is when looking for furniture. Many furniture stores, normally when having a sale, will offer zero percent for twelve, twenty-four, or thirty-six months or some similar deal. To do this, you will get a loan from the finance company the furniture company has partnered with for this deal. In this example, I will use a twelve-month period of no finance charges. Do the math ahead of time to see how much you can afford in your monthly budget over the time of the no-financing deals. Then multiply this amount by eleven, not twelve. This is your total budget for the furniture. After you buy the furniture, you will then be able to pay off the loan in eleven months. This gives you a one-month cushion in paying it off before the interest charges hit. This cushion is important because in most deals like this, the fine print in the loan may allow the loan company to apply all the interest charges that would have been applied from the beginning of the loan if the loan is not paid off completely by the end of the zero percent (promotional) term. I you pay off a loan like this before any interest can be charged, you have helped your credit history by paying off a loan and you didn't have to pay any interest to do it. A similar method may also be used if you need to finance certain dental procedures.

A small way to help with your cash flow is using coupons. This may not sound like it can help much, but they can add up. If you spend thirty minutes gather coupons you can use, either by clipping them from the Sunday paper or using your favorite app, and you save $10.00 when you go grocery shopping every week that is a rate of $20.00 an hour or an extra $520.00 per year. These funds can be used to pay down loans faster, which will save interest and finance charges in the long run, or they can be used to save up for a larger down payment on a future loan. Some people complain about big business nickeling and diming them for every little thing. There is a reason they do that—it works. You can use the same strategy to help yourself save.

How do debit cards aka check cards work?

| The short answer: |

A debit card is used to withdraw funds directly from your checking account. This is why some financial institutions will call them check cards. This is also an effort to prevent confusion with credit cards. Merchants will normally process them in the same manner as a credit card. They can also be used to make purchases using the PIN (person identification number) that is associated with the cardholder and the card number. This option is not typically used online. Instead, they are processed like a credit card and use a security number that is on the back of the card.

| The long answer: |

The debit card is a very versatile financial instrument. Its main function is to help the account holder to make purchases, with the funds for that purchase coming directly from their checking account. While the end result is the same, the transactions completed on your debit card can be processed in two main methods. The first method is called a signature-based transaction. This method treats the card similar to a credit card and is processed by a credit card processor, but the transaction is routed to your financial institution who then routes the transaction to your checking account. The second is called a PIN-based transaction. This method treats your debit card like an ATM card and routes the transaction through an ATM network before it gets to your financial institution.

The signature-based transaction is called this because you normally have to sign for the transaction the same way you would for a credit card. These transactions are also referred to as a swipe transaction. This is because, until recently, a debit card needed to be swiped though a card reader to have the information on the magnetic strip on the back of the card read by the card reader. New technology now uses a chip embedded in the front of the card to complete these types of transactions. This method is a bit slower for the transaction to be completed at the cash register but is much more secure for everyone involved because it creates a one-time authorization that cannot be reused. Most cards in the United States now have both a magnetic strip on the back and a chip on the front. It will take some time, but the strip will go away and the chip with be the only option for this type of transactions. This is already the case in many places outside of the United States. This is because they have few card networks to upgrade. A major step toward completing the conversion from the magnetic strip on the back of your debit or credit card to the chip on the front of your card will be when the change is made at gas stations and convenient stores for pay at the pump transactions. This will take a long time and cost these merchants both time and money.

Processing signature-based transactions after the authorization is received can be done one of two ways. These are batch processing and real-time processing. They both start the same way and get an authorization for a transaction to your account with your debit card and this puts a temporary hold on your account for the authorized amount. The amount put on hold can be different from the final posting amount but is normally not unless the transaction is at certain types of merchants. See the section on credit cards for more detail about authorization amounts and posting amounts. With batch processing, the merchant holds the final transaction information until it has a large batch of them to transmit to the card processor. This is usually done on a daily basis. A smaller retailer will do it this way to save on processing charges because they may be charged for each transmission of the information. A larger retailer may choose to not to process it this way, but to use the real-time option. This process is very similar, but instead of waiting until a batch is created for all the

HOW MONEY WORKS

day's transaction, they will send the information every few hours. For example, all the transaction done at a major retailer between 1:00 PM and 3:00 PM may be transmitted at 4:00 PM. This will allow for quicker deposits to the merchant account for the purchases made at their stores. It cost them more on processing charges, but it is worth it to them to have the cash ready for their business needs, such as quicker inventory turnover. From the point of view of the account holder, the timing of the hold (the authorization) on their account is no different between these two methods, but there is a difference in the timing of the posting. If the financial institution that issued the debit card does not have real-time processing, then the hold may last longer because they will be posting by batch and their process will only send them a file once per day to post all their debit card transactions. For example, if you complete a debit card purchase at a retailer at 9:00 AM for $30 dollars, the hold will be put on your account at the time of the transaction, but the transaction will not post to your account until the process sends the file. This could be as late as 5:00 PM the next business day. If both the retailer and your financial institution have real-time processing, this same transaction will most likely post to your account within two or three hours. You may be wondering, why does this matter? Well, in most cases, it may not matter to you as the account holder, but it is possible it could when making certain types of purchases. These types of purchases may include buying gas at the pump or booking a hotel room. Let's look at the gas pump example first. This will most likely not be much of an issue if you keep track of your checking account balance. Most pay at the pump transactions will authorize $1.00 and create a hold on your account for this much and then post the amount of your actual purchase. Where this can cause a problem is if you are low on funds and need to get gas and then you make another purchase. If you have $20 in your checking account and get $15 worth of gas, the hold is for only $1.00 and your account will show you still have $19 available in your account. The reality is you only have $5 available. Now you stop in to get a quick lunch for $8.00 and the transaction goes through with no problem because of the $19 available showing in your account. Then both of the transactions post and your account is now overdrawn by $3.00. Overdrawing your account is very expensive and should be avoided if at all possible. Another way a pay at the pump transaction can be an issue is when gas prices become really high. When this happened during the "great recession," at least one convenience store company that sold gas at one of the lowest prices in the market changed the authorization amount from $1.00 to $75.00. Now under the same situation as above, you would not even be able to make the gas purchase because your card would be declined for insufficient funds. This is a very frustrating situation that caused many complaints to financial institutions because the account holders thought their card was not working correctly and they wanted their bank or credit union to fix it. The truth was that the system was working correctly, but the increased authorization amount by the merchant caused the card to be declined. This situation may not happen very often when making a purchase at a gas pump, but where it can cause an issue is when booking a hotel room. A hotel may run the authorization for a much larger amount than the expected room charges. For example, if you are just staying one night, they may run an authorization for the charges for that night plus another $50. If you are planning to stay for multiple nights, this can add up quickly. Remember, this is just an example. Each hotel has its own policy and procedures when it comes to these authorizations. Most hotels and some other merchants will call them preauthorizations. If you have already prepaid for the room as is normally the case when booking online, the hotel will still want to get a card from you to cover any incidental charges that you may have while you are staying with them. This does add a level of convenience for you while you are there, but it also puts a hold on your checking account if you are using a debit card. This prevents you from spending this amount even though the funds are still in your account. This is why I recommend to not use a debit card at a hotel but to use a credit card instead. With a credit card, the authorization will lower your available credit, but your credit limit on your credit card will normally have more room than the cash in your checking account.

    Here are few things that most banks, credit unions, and credit cards processors may not want you to know about authorizations.

First, a little good news: they do expire. The authorization hold normally is removed when the transaction is completed and posts to your checking account. Even if for some reason the transaction is not completed, the authorization hold should be removed. This is normally done within three days of the original authorization. Next, different merchants have different codes and the card processors can use this information to treat transaction differently. For example, if the transaction is from a hotel or car rental company, the time frame for the authorization to expire can be longer. This is because the likelihood of staying at a hotel or renting a car lasting more than three days is high. Finally, these holds can be removed by your financial institution. This is very rare and some hoops will need to be jumped through to make it happen. If an authorization from a hotel, rental car company, or other merchant that has longer authorization holds need to be removed the financial institution will most likely require something in writing from that merchant. An example of this would be a hotel authorization for incidentals. You may not have had any, or you may have paid cash when you checked out. In order for the authorization hold to be removed, your financial institution may require permission from the general manager of the hotel in writing on their letterhead. The purpose of this is to prevent you from overdrafting your checking account and to protect the bank or credit union from any violations of their card-processing agreements.

 A PIN-based transaction uses a four-digit personal identification number to verify the cardholder to the card system. The PIN-based transaction was around before debit cards were. When ATMs were invented so was the ATM card. Some of these are still used, but not many because your debit card can complete the same function. PIN-based transactions are normally used to withdraw cash from an ATM but can also be used for purchases. The main difference is, if you want to get cash back from a transaction, you have to use a PIN-based transaction and not a signature-based transaction. For example, if you are buying groceries and you want to pay for your items and get $20.00 in cash as well, people use to write a check for the total plus the $20.00. Now they can use their debit card as a PIN transaction and you may be given the option to get cash back. This depends on the merchant. Some merchants, like small dollar stores, will only accept PIN-based transactions and not signature-based transactions. The reason for this is that the interchange rate, for PIN-based transactions, are normally lower than the interchange rate for signature-based transactions. With a lower interchange rate for PIN-based transactions, most merchants will prefer for you to pay this way, and the banks and credit unions that issue the cards would prefer you to pay with a signature-based transaction. Now you may wonder, why don't the merchants "encourage" shoppers to pay this way? The answer is it would most likely violate the card-processing agreement they have with the major credit card companies that they sign so they can take payment via the card in the first place. Now that you know this and if you have your checking account at not-for-profit financial institution, aka a credit union, you can help them out by using the signature-based option. For more information on interchange rates, see the section on credit cards.

There are also other ways a debit card can also be used to complete transactions ways by the account holder. One of the other major uses of a debit card is as an ATM (automated teller machine) card. When using the debit card this way, you can not only withdraw cash from your checking account, you may also be able to withdraw funds from a savings account that is also linked to the card. If you do have a saving account, or other accounts linked to the card, you would also be able to transfer funds between the accounts. A true ATM can also take deposits. It is best to only make deposits with an ATM that is owned and operated by the financial institution where your account is located. The ATMs that do not take deposits and mostly just let you withdraw money from your account are not truly ATMs and are call cash dispense machines. If you think about it, it makes sense to not call these machines ATMs because you can do much more than just withdraw funds from your account with a teller at a bank or credit union branch. Most of the types of transactions done at an ATM can now be done online or with an app on a mobile device. Even depositing checks can be done this way now and the funds can be credited to your account very quickly. This is the way that the banks and credit unions prefer transactions to be done because the processing charges are much less per transaction for them. They don't have to print you a receipt for the transaction, pay the ATM network processing charges, and it minimizes the communication charges. The cost of the paper receipt and the ATM network processing charges are greater than the cost of processing an online transaction. The difference may be pennies or even less, but when you multiply that difference over thousands of transactions, or even millions of transactions for larger banks, the cost of processing all these transactions adds up really fast. This is especially true with the communication charges. If you use an ATM on a regular basis, then you know about surcharges. These charges can be different from machine to machine and are mainly collected to pay the different ATM networks for transferring the information about your transaction from the ATM back to the financial institution where your account is located. These costs are paid to the network by your financial institution. There are many different networks that transmit this data, and in order for your card to work, your financial institution and the ATM have to be members of that network. The choice of which network is used for your transaction is prioritized by your financial institution. If you look at that back of your debit card, you may see some other logos at the bottom of the card. These are the logos for the networks your financial institution is a member of. The order, from left to right, may also determine which network your transaction attempts to use first. If the machine you are trying to use does not belong to the first network, then the machine will know to try to route your transaction through the next network and so on. You can also tell if your transaction should work before attempting a transaction because the ATM itself normally has these same logos posted on it. These networks are why you can have your account at a small credit union or local community bank and use your card almost anywhere in the country. This includes doing withdraws from ATMs at convenience stores or at grocery stores, or even someplace you may not normally see an ATM like a courthouse building. Places like these also share in the cost of communication of the transaction. They receive a portion of the surcharges you pay for making the transaction at their machine. The network will pay them their portion, normally once a month for the prior month, but they have to pay for the communication method used at their location. They will have to provide internet access for the machine or as most due an old-fashioned phone line. These are also called landlines or POTS lines. POTS stand for plain old telephone service or plain ordinary telephone service. Yes, it can be hard to image, especially when it comes to your money, but many computers still communicate by phone lines. The good news is once the data is received by the network, they speed up the communication with much faster methods of communication.

Another way to use a debit is to use it for what is called reoccurring debits. A reoccurring debit is a regular transaction that takes place at regular interval. This is normally for the same amount each time and most likely on a monthly basis. A good example of this would be a gym membership. These transactions are treating differently from normal debit card transactions. The authorization is not rerun every month but is considered by the card processor to have already been authorized and will send the transaction to post to your checking account. This type of transaction will post to your account even if the funds are not currently available. If the funds are not available, your financial institution will overdraw your account when the transaction posts.

There are a couple of other cards that work similar to debit cards and look a lot like them. They are gift cards with a major credit card company logo on them and reloadable debit cards. The gift card is a card that can be used anywhere that accepts cards with the credit card company logo on it. These normally come in fixed amounts like $25 or $50 dollars and are normally not reusable. The reloadable debit cards are different because you can put any amount on them and use them as long as there are funds linked to the card in an account that is not the cardholder's account but an account managed by the financial institution. These two types of cards may have extra fees associated with them depending on the types of transactions and if you try to use them to get cash from an ATM.

How do I manage my debt?

| The short answer: |

Notice that this topic is about managing debt and not eliminating debt. Controlling debt is the basic goal and having no debt at all and being able to live your life the way you choose is the highest level of debt control. Eliminating all debt is not always practical. I like to compare managing debt to swimming. You don't learn to swim by jumping into the deep end of the pool. That being said, there should be a time when the deep end is not intimidating at all and no matter how much money (swimming skill) you have you can always find yourself in trouble or drowning in debt if you are not careful. The best way to "be careful" and properly control and manage your debt is to live within your means and factor in debt payment to your monthly budget and cash flow.

| The long answer: |

After reading the part above that said "live within your means," you are probably thinking: What does that mean? To answer that question, you have to deal with some good news and some bad news. Let's start with the bad news. Your means is most likely limited by your overall income. Also, you have needs that require part of your means and you may have other commitments you have made with your finances. All of this is a nice way of saying you only have so much money and some of it is already going to places that you need to pay. This would include your regular monthly bills such as rent or mortgage, food, electric bill, and maybe a car payment. The good news is you are in control of setting the priorities for your needs and your commitments. After these are set, by you, you are also in control of setting the priorities for the remainder of your means. A couple of examples of these items may include entertainment and traveling.

What "live within your means" does not include is the amount you can borrow or your credit card limits. The amount a lender, including the amount you can spend on your credit card, is not your means, it is the lender's means. The lenders are willing to let you use their money so you will pay them interest and perhaps other fees as well. Of course, this can get a little blurring sometimes. Especially if you need a vehicle to get to work and you need a loan to be able to purchase the vehicle. This is called the real world. Sometimes you have to borrow money when you not only do not want to, but when you had no plans to, and it was definitely not in your budget. More of this will be addressed in the section on saving. I know that may sound strange now, but it will make for since when you get there.

When writing this section, I went back and forth in my head on how to present ideas that would be beneficial to the reader. After a while, I figured the best way would be to show you some ideas and technics that my wife and I have used in our own life that have helped us manage our debt and keep our credit scores on the very high end of the scale. I have listed the ideas and technics by the type of loan. I have also included some types of loans that we have not used and I would recommend avoiding. I will be very clear about that when you get to the point of reading about them. This may make some kinds of lenders a little upset, but this book is for you and not for them.

| Car Loan (a.k.a. Car Note) |

Depending on where you are in life, a car loan can be the biggest loan in your life or it can just be one of big monthly bills you have to pay. Either way, it is definitely an item that should be included in your budget. When young and you need to buy a car because you need reliable transportation to get to work or school, you may need help from a family member for a down payment. You may even need a cosigner. Understand that anyone that helps you in this manner is trusting you with their financial reputation. See the section on cosigning for more on this. When buying a car, whether your first vehicle or not, a down payment is very important. The more you put down, the less you need to borrow; and the less you need to borrow, the lower your payment and interest charges will be.

Car loans are a type of term loan where you are scheduled to make regular payments on a certain date of the month over a certain time frame. This is why you may have payments that are set for say the fifteenth of the month for seventy-two months. With term loans, the lender may even show you an amortization schedule. This shows all of your payments by month and breaks down how much is principle (the funds you borrowed) and how much is interest (the finance charges for borrowing the money for the car). The main thing to know amount amortization schedules is that they are the lenders plan for you to pay back the funds. From your point of view, it is the minimum requirements for you to pay back the funds. Doing the minimum can and will cost you money, no matter what type of loan you have. I have put a list of some things that will help with managing car loans below. Also, reread the sections on cars as it will help with understanding this type of loan better.

| Tips for Car Loans: |

- Round up your monthly payment. (This will help with budgeting and paying the loan off a little faster.)
- Ask for an amortization schedule on a shorter term. (If you get a seventy-two-month loan, ask for a schedule for sixty-six months.) (If the lender charges for this, just find a loan calculator on the internet, maybe even their site.)
- When your car is paid off, keep making payments to yourself. (Put the funds you normally have for your car payment in a separate savings account. This will help you when it is time to put down funds for a new car or for future car repairs.)
- If you have more than one car in your family, try to have only one car payment at a time. (This just makes budgeting easier.)
- Do not pay a loan late, even if you have a "grace" period before you are considered late. (Every day cost you more

interest on the funds you borrow.) (This is called a per diem and lenders use it to calculate future payoff amounts.) (Per diem is Latin for "per day" or "for each day.")
- Continue to shop for the loan. Most people don't think of refinancing a car loan, but it is something worth considering if you can get a lower interest rate without extending the term of your loan. (It still may be worth considering, if it lowers your monthly payment by such a significant amount that it helps the cash flow needs of your budget.)

| Tips for Title Loans: |

- If your car is paid off and you have the title, you can get a loan by using your car title to get a lower rate for funds you may need. Lower as compared to other loans. (Look for these types of loans at a bank or credit union and not at a title loan company. There are many other costs and fees when using a title loan company that will make this type of loan much more expensive.)
- You should still shop around for title loans just like any other kind of loans. (You don't have to use the same place for the title loans as you did for your original car loan.)
- When shopping around for the funds, consider other types of loans as well. (Personal loans will most likely be more expensive, but secured loans based on the deposited funds in your savings account or a certificate of deposit may result in a lower interest rate.)
- Use of title loans should be rare but may be a better option than carrying a credit card balance at a much higher interest rate.

| Tips for Personal Loans or Personal Lines of Credit: |

- Personal loans and personal lines of credit are unsecured and because of that have higher rates, but the interest rate may be lower than if you applied for a credit card.

- A personal loan is a term loan, just like a car loan, but without the collateral. You can use the same idea of a shorter amortization schedule to pay this loan off earlier than the scheduled term of the loan.
- A personal line of credit is not a term loan, but it may need to be renewed after a number of years. This is determined by the lending institution. Other than that, it works like getting a cash advance on a credit card. Interest starts the day you take a draw of the funds. These may be good for financial emergencies, especially if you don't have a home equity line of credit.

| Credit Cards: |

- It is a good idea not to carry balances on credit cards, especially store credit cards. The interest rates on store credit cards can be and normally are over 20%.
- If you do carry a balance on a credit card, consider looking into a balance transfer to another card. Some lenders will give you a lower introductory rate or balance transfer rate for a period of time, and sometimes even a 0% rate for a short time. Be careful of transfer fees and the timing of when the regular rate starts to apply to the balance.
- If carrying a balance, pay more than the minimum. Paying the minimum may not even cover the interest charges if your balance is too high. Credit card issuers have to tell you the order that they apply your payment to what is due. Normally, this is to fees first, if any, then to interest, then the balance of cash advances and purchases. These balances are separated and your payment can be split between the two with the balance with the highest rate given a higher priority. This can also happen with balance transfers. You could possibly have multiple balances being charged different rates on one credit card. You could have cash advances, balance transfers, and regular purchases all with different interest rates; and if you have multiple balance transfers

done at the different times, your credit card issuer was running a promotion you could have multiple balance transfers with different interest rates.

- Avoid cash advances. There is no delay or grace period on paying interest on cash advances with a credit card. Interest is charged from the day you get the advance. Cash advances use to be done via credit card checks. These are rare now and normally have to be requested from the credit card processor. These checks are linked to your credit card and instead of clearing your checking account they add to the cash advance balance on your credit card. Some card issuers may even charge a higher rate on cash advances than on purchases. Things like this is why it is important to read the disclosers and user agreements. If you do a cash advance with a credit card at an ATM, the owner of the ATM and the credit card issuer may be able to charge you a fee. Don't use a PIN for a credit card. If you are issued one, and it is sent to you vial mail, shred it. There are other transactions the credit card process may treat as cash advances. A few of these are the following: buying gift cards or prepaid debit cards, buying travelers' checks, purchasing foreign currency, and gambling transactions. This may or may not include buying lottery tickets.

| Courtesy Pay—A Loan by Another Name: |

- Courtesy pay is normally a reference to a program where a financial institution pays an ACH transaction, a check, or authorizes a debit card transaction on your checking account when you don't have enough funds for the transaction. For example, if you only have $50 in your checking account and a check attempts to clear for $60 the bank or credit union will clerk the check and not return it. Then they will charge you a fee for paying the check. This is normally about the same amount as their returned check or NSF (insufficient funds) fee. The good part for you, the consumer, is that you don't have to pay a returned check to the merchant you may have written the check to. For debit cards, it will authorize the $60 and charge the fee when it posts. If the courtesy pay fee is $35, your checking account will now be negative $45. The $35 fee is a very expensive charge for the financial institution allowing you to use $10 of their money. Courtesy pay may be marketed with other names, such as overdraft privilege.

- Most courtesy pay programs require you to have checking account that has a minimal amount of a direct deposit. In other words, if you don't have a direct deposit of at least "x" amount, the courtesy pay or overdraft privilege will not be offered to you. If it has been offered to you in the past and your direct deposit drops below the "x" amount, then the privilege may be revoked. Most banks or credit unions will set this amount internally and will not want to discuss it with the consumer. Some may not even tell their branch staff the amount of the minimum direct deposit. Since not everyone is on the same pay schedule, with some people being paid weekly, some biweekly, some semimonthly, and even some once per month most financial institutions will base this minimum direct deposit amount based on each month. They may, in some cases, exclude direct deposits from their calculation that are not pay related if they occur less frequently than once per month.
- Courtesy pay programs may work with an ACH transaction or a check, but not a debit card transaction if you have not opted in for debt card transactions. You will be required to opt in to what your financial institution may call "everyday debit card transactions." This is a personal preference, but if you do not opt in and you try to make a debit card transaction that exceeds your available fund, the transaction may be denied. Some people may find this embarrassing, but in my opinion, paying the courtesy pay or overdraft privilege fee would be much more unpleasant.

Student Loans:

- Student loans have changed over the years, but the point is still to help people obtain financing to pay for a college degree or certification from a trade school. Paying regular payments on your student loans is very important, but the interest is different than other loans. The interest is deductible on the front of your tax return. It is almost as if you didn't make the money you pay in interest. Of course, this is taxes we are talking about, so your deduction has limitations. See a tax profession for more details or just read the instructions for a 1040 tax form.
- Start paying on your student loans while you are still in school. Usually, the payments are delayed until after graduation, but they will take payments and every dollar you pay is a dollar you did not borrow for the next twenty years. This will save you a bunch of interest over the period of time that it will take you to pay off the loan. This will also help you pay off your student loans much faster.
- Lenders will look to sell your loan depending on the market. You should have the same attitude and look at refinancing opportunities. If interest rates are going down, you could find another student loan lender that will help you save money on interest charges.

Payday Loans:

- These loans are dependent on your next paycheck. Avoid these if at all possible. The fees can pile on and can end up causing you lots of problems.
- Payday lenders require access to your checking account information and will keep hitting it until they get their money. If you close the account or the lender cannot get their principle or fees from you, they will not hesitate to take you to court and sue you.

Mortgage Loans:

- I will go into more details about mortgage loans in the next chapter but wanted to give you a couple of items here too. Always try to pay a little extra each month on your mortgage that will all go to the principle balance of the loan, which will help you pay off the loan faster. There are two main ideas on how to do this. The first is to add an extra $100, for example, each month. The second is to review your mortgage statement from the prior month and take note of how much of your payment went to principle and how much went to interest. Like all loans, the interest part will be higher at the beginning of the loan than at the end of the loan; but with a mortgage, the part of your payment applied to the interest will be higher than the principle portion. The difference is how much extra you add each month to the payment. This way you are paying at least as much in principle as in interest. This is a fast way of paying down the loan. This can be done with other loans as well.
- After some time goes by and equity is built up in the home, you can use this to obtain a second mortgage or a home equity line of credit, also called a HELOC. Be careful with these loans, especially if they have adjustable rates. If the Federal Reserve Bank increases the overnight rate, they charge financial institutions for the money they may need to borrow from the Fed then the rate will most likely be increasing on your loan. There may be a delay in this increase and you may not notice it in one or two statement cycles. Most adjustable rate mortgages or home equity lines of credit are based on the prime rate. Although most financial institutions can set their own "prime" rate, it is normally the Fed fund rate at the below link plus 3%. Try to stay away from adjustable rate loans of any kind when rates are showing a pattern of increasing over the last twelve months. You can take a look at this on the Federal Reserve Bank website below to see these patterns at any

time: https://www.federalreserve.gov/monetarypolicy/openmarket.htm
- In a situation where interest rates show a pattern of decreasing, shop around. Look for lower rates all the time. Refinancing your mortgage can save you a lot of money if the interest is at least 1% lower than you are already paying. Even if the required payment goes down, you can continue to make your payment at the same amount as your old loan. Be careful with closing costs though. Compare an amortization schedule of your potential new mortgage loan's total interest over the life of the loan to an updated amortization schedule of your current mortgage loan. If the savings in interest expense is not more than the closing costs, you have to pay; it may not be worth the time and effort to refinance, even at the lower rate.

When should I buy a house?

| The short answer: |

Many people ask themselves this question about buying a home. When is very important because it is such a large and long-term purchase. The "when" is not just about when the buyer can afford a house. It is also about when are home prices and the market in the favor of the buyer over the seller, when are mortgage interest rates low, and when are property values are reasonable? The key is, of course, the buyer being able to afford a house. What does this really mean? A good start to being able to put a good-sized down payment. This would be about 20% of the purchase price of the house. This may be something you heard before, but there is also a second part. The second part has to do with the monthly payment. If your monthly payment can be covered by one-quarter of your household take-home pay in a given month, this means you can afford the home from a cash flow basis. Managing the mortgage loan balance and the mortgage loan payment are both important when it comes to when you can afford to buy a house.

| The long answer: |

So, let's expand on being able to afford a house. The 20% down payment idea is a good place to start. Besides the point of any loan being that the more you put down, the less you have to borrow, which means you will have lower interest payments over the life of the loan. You will also avoid PMI. PMI stand for private mortgage insurance. The point of private mortgage insurance is to protect the lender from potential default of the borrower. When the amount borrowed is greater than 80% of the value of the property that is the collateral of the mortgage the chance of default or failure to pay as agreed is statistically higher. Even though PMI is to protect the lender, you, as the borrower, pay for it each month as part of your monthly mortgage payment. It is normally percentage of the loan balance. This percentage can be normally at least 0.5% but also can be as high as 2%. This means on a mortgage that carries a balance of $200,000 you could pay as much as $4,000 or more extra in the first year of the loan. The lender will tell you about the need for PMI when you apply for the mortgage, but there is a real good chance that when your mortgage balance drops below the 80% value of the property, they most likely will not remind you that you can have it removed from your monthly payments. This is really on you to keep track of this situation if you find yourself with a mortgage that has PMI. When you drop below the 80%, it may be a good time to look to refinance. If you started with a thirty-year mortgage, this would be a good time to look at moving to a fifteen-year mortgage.

Okay, now that the house has been purchased and you have figured the cost of a mortgage payment into your monthly budget, what is next about being able to afford a house? This is where the continuous work comes in. There are the regular bills that you also need to be able to afford. A few of these include power (electric and/or gas), water, and regular maintenance such as cutting the grass. Yes, you need to factor in all these things, even the small ones. Some of the larger items may include things like dues to a homeowners' association. In some places, these may be included in your monthly mortgage and put into an escrow account similar to an amount for your property taxes. I am not personally a big fan of HOAs (homeowners associations), but some people like them, and they can have some nice benefits. If you are looking at a house to purchase and you have a real estate agent, this is the first question you need to ask about the house. Is there a HOA? If the answer is yes, then there will be many more questions to follow. Being able to afford all of these regular expenses are important to plan for, but perhaps the most important regular expense would be your homeowner's insurance. Speak with an insurance agent before you start looking for a house.

Other items about being able to afford a house is not just the regular bills, but also the things that are unplanned. Being prepared for things to no work is very important to long-term household budgeting. Things break all the time. A few examples are major appliances such as the washer, the dryer, the dishwasher. These are things that you may be able to work around for a little while by going to the laundromat or by doing dishes by have for a while, but then comes the big things you will need to be prepared for. A couple of these would include the heating and cooling system and the roof. Yes, I said roof. In case no one has told you, a roof has a shorter life span than the rest of the house. A regular asphalt shingled roof can last twenty to twenty-five years. Annual inspections are not a bad idea.

Running the numbers for the above costs and expenses is a good place to start when it comes to thinking about buying affording a home. The next step is finding the people that can help you in the process. These people may include a mortgage loan officer at a bank or credit union, a real estate agent, and an insurance agent. These people need to be identified before you start looking for a house. Keep in mind that these people all want you to be able to buy the house. This is a big one-time transaction for you, but they make their living by helping these transactions happen. The mortgage loan officer will ask you many questions, just like for any loan, but the most important is, how much will you be looking to put down on the house? The real estate agent usually makes around 3% of the sales price. This can cost the seller around 6%. The payment for your real estate agent and their real estate agent comes out of the proceeds. This is why some people try to sell their own homes first. The next person to talk with is your insurance agent. If you already have car insurance with an agent, they may be able to give you a discount for having more than one policy with them. Homeowners' insurance is very important when it comes to being prepared. Storms can happen anywhere and damage your home, but always remember homeowners' policies do not cover floods. Flood insurance is a separate policy. This is part of the discussion you need to have with your insurance agent. After you have identified a house and before you make an offer, you will want to make sure a home inspector takes a look at it before you buy it. This is an expense you would want to pay yourself. It is very important that the inspector works for you and nobody else. He should provide you a written report of his findings, but don't hesitate to accompany the inspector while he is doing the inspection and ask questions as you go along.

Do I really need life insurance?

The short answer:

Some people say it is rude to answer a question with a question, but in this case, I think it is appropriate. To answer the question of the need for life insurance, all you need to do is ask yourself one question: Am I alive? If the answer to this question is yes, then one day you will not be alive and that is where life insurance comes into the picture. No matter your personal or religious preferences of how your final expenses are handled, there will be final expenses to handle. Life insurance is therefore not for you but for the people you have asked to be in charge of handling your final wishes after you leave this life.

The long answer:

Here it sounds like the short answer may be the only answer you really need, but there is more information you can use. You may think the life insurance funds are made to pay for funeral expenses and that is the end of it, but with proper planning, it can work out better than that. Let's look at some of the ways it can work out better for you and your loved ones.

First, let's look at some of the major expenses related to a funeral. A few of these would include funeral home services, a vault and casket, a burial plot, and a marker or headstone. For the funeral home services, many of them have prepayment plans, also called preneed plans. You may be able to pay for their services in full ahead of time or you may be able to make installment payments over a period of time. Either way, this will allow more of your life insurance benefits to go where you want them to go instead of to the funeral home because you have already taken care of that expense. Now this sounds really good if you don't plan on moving again and you know for sure that the funeral home itself will be in business longer than you will be. Caskets, vaults, and markers can also be prepaid for before they are needed. Since these things change and you don't know the costs of these goods and services in the future, you can also open a POD account at your local credit union or bank. These payable on death accounts are completely separate from any other planning you may do. You tell the credit union or bank who the beneficiary of the account is and when you pass away all they have to do is bring in a copy of your death certificate, and they give them the funds. If you have someone that you trust enough to be the executor of your will, it would most likely be this person and you can ask them to use these funds for your funeral expenses.

The one item that is different from the rest of the other funeral expenses is the burial plot. This is an actual piece of land that can grow in value and can be sold. There are very few places in the world were more land is being made so the chances of your burial plot increasing in value over the long-term is very good. I would recommend that if you do no other planning of final expenses, buy at least one burial plot for every living member of your household. These plots, if not needed, can always be sold, or you can leave them to those you choose to in your will. Many cemeteries have installment plans that require no financing at all. Cemeteries will use the funds you pay them for normal operating cost and most will put the funds in an endowment or trust that will help fund the cemetery operations before and after it is full to capacity.

When your final expenses are covered by other planning, the proceeds from your life insurance policy can be used for many other options by the beneficiaries. Everyone has different circumstances in their lives, but some of these uses of these proceeds could be to replace income that you have been providing or pay off debt. The main issue that can face those you have lost a loved one, especially if that lost was earlier than expected, is the loss of income that individual provided and how that affects the cash flow of the entire household. The life insurance proceeds can be used to replace the cash flow over time by using only what is needed to replace the income or by paying down the debt that was being paid with the lost income. Other items the life insurance proceeds can be used for by the beneficiaries when you have planned ahead and paid for final expenses included education expenses, down payments on large purchases such as a house or car, or paying down their debt.

Before you purchase life insurance for yourself or other members of your family, the key is to find an insurance agent you can trust. The insurance agent is a salesman first. This is how they make a living, so do your own research as well. When you do this, you will find out about term life insurance, the most basic type of life insurance that lasts for an agreed period of time. You will also learn about whole life insurance, which can grow in value, but this can take some time. These two are the most common types, and they may have subcategories as well. This is why it is important to find an expert that you can trust with this knowledge.

When should I start saving for retirement?

| The short answer: |

Everyone has asked themselves this question, most likely more than once. There are a number of points of view on this, but there are very few financial professionals that know anything amount money who would tell you not to be saving for retirement when you have finished your education and have started working full-time. This kind of retirement savings is put front of mind because of starting to work and most likely your employer will have discussed with you their 401(k) program or other retirement plans they have as an employee benefit. If they have not talked to you about this, ask them as soon as possible.

| The long answer: |

Saving for retirement when you start working full-time is a normal place to start thinking about saving for retirement. You are starting something, your career, and like any journey you are also thinking about the end of the journey or the destination along with the beginning. However, this should be seen as the latest option for beginning your retirement savings. When you start working any job, full-time or part-time, the federal government requires your employer to withhold funds from your paycheck for the future Social Security payments you will receive in retirement and requires them to match this amount as your employer. For example, if you are paid $10.00 per hour and work 20 hours for a pay period at your part-time job, your gross pay (amount before withholdings and deductions) will be $200.00 and your employer will be required to withhold from your paycheck 6.2% or $12.40. This does not include amounts for future Medicare benefits or any income tax withholdings for federal, state, or local income taxes. Your employer will also have to contribute the same amount when they remit or pay the Social Security amounts for this pay period. So, even if you don't have the necessary income to start saving for retirement, the government will force you and your employer to start saving for it by imposing these taxes from your very first paycheck of any kind. These are funds that you may have earned, but you have no control over. It may be a good idea to start your retirement saving at the same time with funds that you do have control over. This does not have to be a 401(k) or an IRA, especially if you are not working full-time yet, but you can still start saving for retirement in other ways. One way would be the old-fashioned savings account. Another would be to start paying down any student loans early so that you will have more to put into your employer sponsored retirement plan when you are working full-time.

The main idea for saving for retirement is to make sure you will have enough money to last you the rest of your life. Some people have the attitude that Social Security will take care of that. The reality is that Social Security payments will most likely not cover the expenses of the lifestyle you have when you retire. This can even be the case if you have paid off all your debt by the time you retire, which, I would highly recommend doing, no matter what kind of retirement plans or savings you may have. Another reason Social Security will most likely not cover your expenses is due to regular increases in the cost of living. Social Security payments will have increases along the way, and they may be called cost of living increases or cost of living adjustments, but the chances of these increases actually matching the actual increase of the cost of living and other inflationary items is very slim. The best way to ensure that you have enough income for retirement is to look beyond the idea of saving and into income-producing assets. One of the biggest fears of retirement is that you will outlive your money. This happens when a retiree uses up all their retirement savings before they die. This is not a good situation to be in. The idea of income-producing assets is also called living of the interest. This doesn't always have to literally be interest earned on cash in a retirement or savings account. It can also be money earned by other assets. A couple of examples would be rental income from houses and dividend income from stocks or bonds. These items can be used to pay for regular living expenses in retirement or just as a supplement that can make sure that you outlive your retirement savings.

Okay, at this point, you may be asking yourself, what is the point of a retirement program such as a 401(k) or an IRA? Other than having money to live on when you retire, the other main reason is the income tax benefit. For example, when you have a regular 401(k), you don't pay money on the income when you earn it, and you see the deduction for it on your paycheck. You are taxed on these funds when you receive them from your retirement plan as retirement income. The idea is that you will be in a lower income tax bracket at that point, and you will pay much less income taxes on these funds in retirement than you would have while you were working. The Roth version of a 401(k) works the other way. You pay the income taxes now on the amount deducted from your paycheck, along with the rest of your earnings. The plus side of that is these amounts have already been taxed, and you will not have any income tax liability related to these funds when you are retired. Choosing which one is best for you can be a hard decision, but sometimes it can be an easy one because your employer, usually the one that is paying for the administration of the plan, only offers one plan. The is normally a regular version of the 401(k) plan.

How do I save money?

| The short answer: |

This is another question people ask themselves often. The first step to answering the question is to define what you mean by saving money. There are two different ways of looking at saving money. Do you want to spend less money for the things you buy? This is the conserving meaning. Or, do you want to save money for a large purchase such as a car, house, college, or a nice vacation? This is the building-up meaning. The good news is these two processes of saving can be combined to help you have more control over your money.

| The long answer: |

First, let's talk about saving money from the conserving point of view. Basically, this means you don't want to spend more than you need to on purchases. To increase the chances of not spending more than you need or want to on everyday purchases, there are a few things that you will want to do and a few things you will not want to do.

One of the major things you will want to do to conserve the money you spend is to use coupons. Some people may think this is a waste of time and an inconvenience. Frankly, I used to think that too, but my wife showed me how much you can save, especially on groceries. Using coupons along with most grocery store frequent-shopper programs, you can save a very high percentage on your grocery bill. You can see this saving at the bottom of the receipt. Yes, there are catches to doing this. First, you have to give your information to be part of the frequent-shopper program. Second is that you have to carefully look at the prices on the items as you shop. Some of the sale items in the store may only apply if you are part of the frequent-shopper program and you buy a certain number of items of that product. Getting coupons to use is of course the beginning of this process. There are many places online to get coupons. You know the products you like and you can even look for coupon apps for your smartphone. Then, of course, is the old-fashioned way, the Sunday paper. You can subscribe to the Sunday paper only and use the coupons you cut from the advertisements that come with it. If you use the coupons to their full potential, they will more than pay for the cost of the paper.

Another way to conserve the money you send is to be careful with the way you spend your money. You do not want to get in the habit of borrowing money to make every day or regular purchases such as for food, gas, or clothing. A good way of doing this is to make these purchases with cash or your debit card and not your credit card. If you choose to use your credit card for the rewards or for other reasons, make sure you can pay it off before the credit card issuer starts charging you interest.

Now let's talk about the building-up meaning of saving money This can be difficult for some people because they see their savings balance increasing and they feel the need to spend it. The old phrase for this is that the money is burning a hole in their pocket. The place to start with this type of saving or building up of funds is to identify what you want to save for. This could be that vacation you and the family really need to take, or it could the down payment for the new car that you know you are going to need in a couple of more years. The next step is to find a separate place to keep the money that you are saving. A really good idea for this is an account at a credit union. Most credit unions have regular savings and checking accounts as subaccounts under one membership number. Many of them have the ability to have additional subaccounts that you can use as extra savings accounts. You may even be able to change the name of the subaccount to match the name of the item you are saving for. The next step is to automate the savings process. Many people have loan payments that are automated; you can do the same with your savings. If your paycheck is deposited directly to your checking account, you can ask your employer's payroll department if they can have a dollar amount sent to another account. For example, if your total net pay is $1,000 and you want $200 to go to your savings account, most employers with direct deposit can do that. From that point, if you are using the credit union scenario above, you can have the $200 split into different subaccounts for different items you may be saving for. Another example would be if you have a car payment that is automatically withdrawn from your account and you pay off the loan, you can then set it up so these funds are transferred to account or subaccount that you will use in the future as a down payment for your next car. Be careful with this strategy. You may want to use these funds for car repairs but figuring out if it is better to fix the car you have or get a new one can be tricky sometimes. If you plan ahead, you can use this strategy for many other things as well. A few other examples would be a house, home repairs and appliances, medical expenses, or other unexpected expenses related to an emergency situation. Doing this for unplanned events will help your normal life not be financial impacted as much by the unexpected things in life. Finding a way to save for unplanned events can be difficult, but as I mentioned in the short answer, you can combine the conserving of your money with the building up of your funds. The coupon example works very well for this. When you get your receipt from the grocery store or any other store where you have used coupons and the amount you saved is on the bottom of the receipt, you can use that amount as a guide to transfer funds to an account you are using to build up funds. It doesn't have to be the entire amount. You can use half of it or even a smaller percentage as your cash flow need determine.

  When you want to save money, remember these few things. Saving a little bit at a time will add up. The best tool for saving money, whether you do it by conserving it or by building it up, is your attention to the details. Know what you have and know where it is going!

What do I need to know about the employer side?

| The short answer: |

Unlike some of the other topics discussed in this book, this is not a question people ask themselves very often. However, there are a few things you may want to know as an employee just so you have a better understanding of how things work. The simple answer is that when an employer hires and pay someone to work for them, there are many other expenses in addition to the employee's salary or wages.

| The long answer: |

First thing an employer has to figure is how many employees they need to complete the tasks required. This can also may require an organizational chart with the chain of command showing what employees report to what supervisors. Then they need to calculate the appropriate rate of pay for these employees. Research will need to be done to make sure the pay offered to these employees is a competitive pay so the people they hire don't leave soon after being hired. You may be thinking, so what if they leave, they can be replaced, just like anyone else? Most of the time you are correct, but that doesn't account for the lost time in training and the retraining of the new employee. These things cost money and, more importantly, time. Speaking of time, now comes the part that can take up more time than any employer wants. This is the time to post the jobs, review résumés, conduct interviews, and make job offers to the candidates. Then if the job is accepted, there is the time needed to complete the payroll forms, the benefits if offered, and reviewing of the company handbook, company policies, and other orientation items. These items can be mixed in with the training process depending on the assigned tasks of the position but all are time where the employee is being paid and not doing their normal tasks.

Next are the payroll costs that are needed just for having employees at all. This includes payroll processing, payroll taxes, the administration of these payroll taxes, and other taxes and items that are withheld. No matter where the employer processes payroll themselves, also called in-house processing, or they outsource it to a payroll company to handles many of these tasks, it still cost money just to pay their employees.

One of the biggest of these costs are the payroll taxes. These include four main types of taxes depending on your state and locality. These are Social Security tax, Medicare tax, the federal unemployment tax (FUTA), and the state unemployment tax (SUTA). Combined the Social Security tax and the Medicare tax are call FICA. This stands for federal insurance contributions act. This act requires both the employee and the employer to contribute to the Social Security retirement fund and the Medicare (hospital insurance benefits fund) for older Americans. Others may also qualify for these government payments. The current Social Security tax rate is 6.2% for the employer and 6.2% for the employee. The current Medicare tax rate is 1.45% for the employer and 1.45% for the employee. From the employer's ID, this adds 7.65% of your gross pay to the cost of employing someone. For example, if you are paid $10 per hour for a forty-hour work week and are paid every two weeks, your total gross pay for your paycheck would be $800.00. This would cost the employer and additional $61.20 ($800.00 times 7.65%). See the chart below for how this cost can grow with the number of employees. An employer with 1,000 employees could hire 62 more people if they did not have to pay this tax. This is one option if employers didn't have to pay this tax, others would include, increasing pay rates for current employees or contributing additional amounts to employee retirement plans. Any combination of this could be done without damage to the company's net income. Some would say that the Social Security part of the FICA tax has been made antiquated and obsolete due to 401(k), IRAs and other plans that have better rates of return. These plans are much better managed as well because the results matter to those managing them. Their reputation and level of success in the business are on the line when they are managing your retirement fund. In other words, they have skin in the game.

	1 Employee	10 Employees	100 Employees	1000 Employees
Annual Gross Pay	$ 20,800.00	$ 208,000.00	$ 2,080,000.00	$ 20,800,000.00
Employer FICA Tax rate	6.20%	6.20%	6.20%	6.20%
Employer FICA Tax	$ 1,289.60	$ 12,896.00	$ 128,960.00	$ 1,289,600.00
Additional FTE at $10/hr possible without Tax	0.06	0.62	6.20	62.00

Notes:

1. Chart shows and average pay rate of $10 per hour for a forty-hour work week for one year.
2. FTE = full-time equivalents (someone working forty hours per week in this example)
3. Employer FICA tax rate used is the rate for the 2018 tax year.

Besides the rates and what the money is paid for, there is another difference between the Social Security tax and the Medicare tax and that there is a limit on the wages that can be taxed for Social Security. The 2018 limit is $128,400. This limit is subject to change by congress for any given future year. There is no wage limit for the Medicare tax. The Medicare tax rate can increase based on the employee's taxpayer's filing status. An additional 0.9% will be required to be withheld from an individual's gross pay if the gross pay exceeds $200,000 in a calendar year regardless of the employee's tax filing status. There is no additional amount for the employer side of the Medicare tax.

Other payroll taxes may include FUTA, the federal unemployment tax, and SUTA, the state unemployment tax depending on what state the employer operates within. Most employers are required to pay this tax quarterly and to file a Form 940. This is the employer's annual federal unemployment (FUTA) tax return. This is to verify that the employer has paid the current FUTA tax rate of 6% on the first $7,000 of wages for each employee during a given year. A small piece of good news related to the FUTA tax is that if an employer has paid state unemployment tax they may receive a credit of up to 5.4%. For more information on the federal unemployment tax please visit the following IRS website: https://www.irs.gov/taxtopics/tc759. The SUTA tax can be a little more complicated than FUTA because of the different rules in each state. Some states have different rates and these rates can be subject to different criteria. A couple of these include the number of people that use to work for the employer that have filed for unemployment and the frequency of paying the SUTA tax late. Some states will not just charge late fees and interest to the employer for paying late but will increase the rate of the tax for a period of time. As with the FUTA tax, there is a small piece of good news with the SUTA tax. States may allow a new employer that has bought the assets of another employer to keep the same SUTA tax rate as the prior employer if they retain a certain percentage of the seller's employees. Please see your state's department of taxation or unemployment commission's website for more information on your state's laws regarding their unemployment tax.

Are there different kinds of banks?

| The short answer: |

This is not something most people think about, but I have included this information just in case it may make a difference to you after you know it. You make think, a bank is a bank. They just want to make money from me just like any other business. This train of thought would be most appropriate for retail banks, but not all "banks." Besides retail banks, there is also central banks, commercial banks, investment banks, and cooperative banks or credit unions.

| The long answer: |

First, let's look at central banks. There is normally one central bank in a country. In the United States, the central bank is the Federal Reserve Bank. It was established by the Federal Reserve Act in 1913. Many of the other types of banks are the customers of the Federal Reserve Bank. The Federal Reserve Bank will help them with the processing of transactions such as ACH, checks, and wires. The Federal Reserve Bank works as the middleman. This way each of the other types of banks do not have to have a financial relationship with each other. They all just need to have a relationship with the Federal Reserve. The Federal Reserve also has financial oversight over the banking industry and provides many types of economic research to the other types of banks and the public. The Federal Reserve is also in charge of the nation's money supply and setting of interest rates. The most well-known interest rate is the federal funds rate. This rate is set by a committee named the Federal Open Market Committee and represents the rate the Federal Reserve can charge other banks for borrowing funds on a short-term basis. In summary, the Federal Reserve has four main tasks and they are the following:

1. Being the bank for other banks and assisting with financial transactions.
2. Supervising banks and other financial institutions by measuring their financial security and well-being.
3. Handling the money supply and interest rates to keep the economy as stable as possible.
4. Providing information on the economy to banks, the government, and to the public.

Next, let's look at commercial banks and retail banks. These are the banks that are in the business to make money by using other people's money. They used to be operated separately from each other, and in some places, they still may be but now there is not much of a difference between the two. They provide most of the same services, such as savings accounts, checking accounts, and many different types of loans. This is why they are normally now considered different divisions of the same bank. Another reason most banks combined their commercial banking business with their retail banking business is volume. There are not as many customers that need the services of the commercial division as there are customers that need the services of the retail division. The commercial banking division of a bank will normally have large commercial accounts. If a large company that is traded on the New York Stock Exchange needs a multimillion-dollar loan to expand its business it would go to the commercial banking division and not the retail banking division. If you are running a small business and need a loan for the same reason, you would most go to the retail division. The retail division is the part of a bank that most people are familiar with, whether this is a bank that you can find in any state in the country or your local community bank.

No matter if the commercial division or the retail division, the main thing to know about these types of banks is they do not make most of their money from the many different services they may provide the customer, the majority is from one type of product and that is *loans*. It's not the fees they may charge for an overdraft; this is to cover their costs of processing and to deter the behavior. It is not the monthly service charges. This may be charge so they can waive it if you get a loan with them. The interest charged on loans is a bank's number one source of income.

Finally, let's look at cooperative banks and credit unions. These are basically the same type of financial institution. They are called cooperative banks in some countries, but in the United States, this type of financial institution is called a credit union. Credit unions operated much like banks but are owned by their members. These are the people that have accounts at the credit union. The account holders elect the volunteer board of directors that make the big financial decisions. These volunteers must have an account at the credit union to be eligible to serve on the board. Credit union elections work on the one-person-one-vote system, so it does not matter how much you have on deposit or how many loans or other services you use at the credit union. Look at the below chart and ask yourself, which one do you think is going be the better situation for an individual account holder at a financial institution?

Financial Institution Type	Owners	Board of Directors	Taxes	Federally Insured
Retail Bank	Stockholders	Paid	For Profit - Taxed	Yes
Credit Union	Account holders	Volunteers	Not-For-Profit	Yes

Notes:

1. Federally chartered credit unions are tax exempt from federal income taxes by IRS code section 501-c-1.
2. State-chartered credit unions are tax exempt from federal income taxes by IRS code section 501c-14.
3. Banks and credit unions are required to have deposit coverage, but do not have to have their deposits federally insured. This is why banks can say: Member FDIC. Private insurance is done by very few financial institutions and is

normally much more expensive. Additional insurance can be purchased for amounts above $250,000.
4. Since credit unions are not-for-profit, they can work together in ways banks cannot. This allows members of one credit union to conduct transactions at another credit union if both are part of the shared branching network. Not all credit unions completely participate in this type of cooperation.

Credit unions officially became separate financial institutions after the passing of the Federal Credit Union Act in 1934. It was signed into law on June 26 by President Franklin D. Roosevelt. This act also established the NCUA or National Credit Union Administration. Today, the NCUA oversees and regulates federally chartered credit union and is responsible for the NCUSIF or the National Credit Union Share Insurance Fund. This is the fund that is used to insure the deposits in credit unions to the federal maximum of $250,000. This is the same amount as the FDIC (Federal Deposit Insurance Corporation) insures for banks. There is one major difference between banks and credit unions when it comes to insurance. During the Great Recession when many financial institutions failed, many banks received a funds from the government to be able to continue operations. This was not the case for credit unions. Credit unions were forced to make difficult financial decisions but did not receive any funds from the government. This is not to say that credit unions did not suffer during the financial crisis. Many were not able to continue and were merged into more successful credit unions by the NCUA. The ones that did continue were required to deposit additional funds into the National Credit Union Share Insurance Fund to make sure the fund would be able to handle any future financial issues.

There are different types of credit unions, but their differences are minor. A credit union is either a federally chartered or state chartered. That is, they are formed under federal law or state law. In some cases, a credit union can change for one to the other, but when they do this, they become a new credit union with a new credit union charter number with the NCUA. Charter numbers are how you can research the financial situation of any credit union at the NCUA website (https://www.ncua.gov/). This is all public information. You can look at their quarterly 5300 Call Report or their quarterly financial performance report.

One of the major changes with the types of credit unions came in 1998 when Congressman Newt Gingrich introduced the Credit Union Membership Access Act, and it was signed into law by then President Bill Clinton. This amendment to the Federal Credit Union Act opened membership to any person who lives, works, attends school, worships, or volunteers in a community that a credit union serves. Credit unions must apply for the type of "community charter," but they are almost always granted. Prior to the Credit Union Membership Access Act, most credit unions memberships were subject to a common bond relationship. For example, employees of a large company could work together to form their own credit union. This is still possible, but is now quite rare, because it is very likely there is a community credit union near them. The common bond relationship can be a little ironic if you look at the history. At one point, the employees of the FDIC formed their own credit union. That must make you think a little.

About the Author

W. Scott Blackmon has been a licensed Certified Public Accountant since October of 2001. After spending a couple of years in the world of public accounting, Scott decided that this type of accounting and the lifestyle required for this type of work was not for him. While studying for the CPA exam, Scott worked at local credit union as the head teller. He was in charge of overseeing the other tellers and the receiving of large cash shipments into the vault. He found the people in the credit union industry to be good people and truly wanting to help others. For this reason, when looking for another position, the credit union industry is the first place he looked. At this point, Scott moved back into the credit union field as the Accounting Manager for a local credit union. A short time later, he was promoted to the Vice President of Accounting. During his combined seventeen years working at credit unions, Scott learned many things about how personal finances actual work from the side of a financial institution. Although credit unions are not-for-profit financial cooperatives, they are run and managed like a bank with only a few exceptions. Scott has now moved on to another career outside of credit unions, but still has the desire to help people with their personal finances. Not the retirement planning and investing strategies that most finance professional are referring to, but the real-world day-to-day aspect of dealing with personal finance. That is why he wrote this book. Knowledge is truly power, and Scott wants to share this knowledge in the hope that those who read it will be able to use this knowledge to help make a better sense of how their money works.

Scott also wanted to include the following personal example of how the knowledge in this book may be able help you. He once applied for a loan with a local financial institution. The person helping him with the loan happened to be the branch manager and had many years of experience helping people with their loans. The loan application was taken and approved, but a curious thing happened when the documents were being printed. One of the documents did not print. This was very puzzling to the branch manager. The document was normally a very helpful one to those seeking loans. It gave advice to help improve your credit score. After searching for a solution for a few minutes, the branch manager noticed that the Vice President of Lending was in the branch and decided to ask for help with the situation. After of few minutes of the Vice President of lending looking over the application, the paperwork, and everything in the computer system, the mystery was solved. No form printed to show how to improve his credit score because his credit score was at 850. This is as high as credit scores go, so there was no need for the document to print.

www.ingramcontent.com/pod-product-compliance
Lightning Source LLC
Chambersburg PA
CBHW021005180526
45163CB00005B/1899